Counting the Days

*Growing your Family's Spirit
by Counting the Omer*

Lea Gavrieli

BenYehuda Press
Teaneck, New Jersey

COUNTING THE DAYS ©2016 Lea Gavrieli. All rights reserved. No part of this book may be used or reproduced in any manner whatsoever without written permission except in the case of brief quotations embodied in critical articles and reviews.

Published by Ben Yehuda Press
122 Ayers Court 1#B
Teaneck, NJ 07666

http://www.BenYehudaPress.com

ISBN13 978-1-934730-49-2

19 18 17 16 / 10 9 8 7 6 5 4 3 2 1   20160508

For my kids, who make every day count.

Through the merit of this work may all beings recognize Omniscience

Counting the Days: A Family Guide to Sefirat Ha-Omer

Preface

What values are most important to us? What is true strength? What constitutes real kindness?

Questions like these seldom come up for discussion in the average twenty-first century life. There are few opportunities for parents and their children to think together about values and spirituality in our always-on, very connected and busy culture,

This books offers a way to take a closer look at our lives. It uses a framework taken from Jewish mystical tradition: counting the 49 days between the holidays of Passover and Shavuot.

This practice originated in the Torah's command to bringing a measure (omer) of barley to the tent of meeting every day for seven full weeks. When the Temple in Jerusalem was destroyed, the ritual of the offering was replaced with a ritual of counting the days and weeks on which the barley would have been offered.

Later, the practice was moved into the spiritual and psychological realm. Mystics used the seven-week cycle of seven days to embark on a journey of spiritual inventory and preparation each spring. This system lets us look within ourselves for our best expressions of holiness as we anticipate and prepare for the festival of Shavuot, which marks the receiving of the Ten Commandments.

The mystical, mindful conception of counting the omer — Sefirat haOmer — provides a map and a direction for thinking about the interplay among the many aspects of our relationships and our day-to-day interactions — with others, with ourselves and with the Divine. Along this journey, we will pass through places where the road narrows into stringency and seriousness, and where it widens to encompass celebration and even great joy. Becoming aware of who we are — and working to get better at it — is part and parcel of the regular daily life of being Jewish. The addition of one more positive command — something more we can do - makes the period of Sefirat haOmer exalted and special. Sefirat haOmer finds a parallel in the blowing of the shofar at morning prayers every day of the month of Elul leading up to Rosh HaShanah; a call to wake up and be more than we have been before.

Judaism is a religion of action: we observe even when our belief wears a little thin. Sometimes, as one of my teachers taught me many years ago, "practice brings belief." Doing, even if you might not believe in this moment, is not inauthentic or hypocritical — it is true Judaism at its finest. So, please join in on this journey. Feel free to write your notes in this book, use it as a map, and then come back and walk this path again next year. Even with the same map, it will be a different journey.

Introduction

וּסְפַרְתֶּם לָכֶם, מִמָּחֳרַת הַשַּׁבָּת, מִיּוֹם הֲבִיאֲכֶם, אֶת-עֹמֶר הַתְּנוּפָה: שֶׁבַע שַׁבָּתוֹת, תְּמִימֹת תִּהְיֶינָה. עַד מִמָּחֳרַת הַשַּׁבָּת הַשְּׁבִיעִת, תִּסְפְּרוּ חֲמִשִּׁים יוֹם; וְהִקְרַבְתֶּם מִנְחָה חֲדָשָׁה, לַיהוָה.

'Count for yourselves, from the day after the holiday, (Pesach), from the day you brought the Omer for waving. It shall be seven complete weeks, and on the day after the end of the seventh week, you will count fifty days and offer a new offering to God' (Lev. 23:15, 16).

What we achieve inwardly will change our outer reality.

—Plutarch

Compared to Passover and Sukkot, Shavuot's description in the Torah is spare. Passover has matza and Sukkot has booths. Shavuot has a calendar. The primary command concerning the holiday is to count the days from the day after the previous holiday, Passover, until 50 days have been counted, and then to bring a new offering to God. On the first day of the count, an offering of barley was brought to the Temple. How much barley? An omer's worth — about three and a half liters, or just shy of a gallon.

With the destruction of the Temple in Jerusalem nearly 2,000 years ago, the barley offering ended — but the counting of the days, in Hebrew Sefirat ha-Omer, continued.

Over time, the nature of the counting, its meaning, and the way we are aware of time and its passage during those days evolved. The original Biblical command gave no particular emotional valence to the counting or to the period between the holidays of Passover and Shavuot. However, Sefirat haOmer became a period of semi-mourning and abstinence from certain joyous activities. Our understanding of the meaning and origin of the aspect of mourning during this period has been diluted and obscured by the passage of time until only the practice of it remains, but it is generally thought that the mourning is connected to a plague which affected the students of Rabbi Akiva, possibly for the sin of disrespecting one another. The plague was said to have ended on the 33rd day of the Omer, which has become the semi-holiday of Lag ba-Omer. This understanding makes the recent evolution of the observance of Sefirat haOmer from simple abstinence to self-examination quite fitting indeed. (We will explore the connection to Rabbi Akiva and his students in greater detail later in the book.)

A critical step in the evolution from counting and mourning to self-examination took place in the city of Tzvat, in northern Israel, in the 16th century. There a group of Kabbalists, experts and practitioners of the Kabbalah, the Jewish mystical tradition, connected the cycle of the Omer to seven of the Divine sefirot. We'll explore the sefirot in detail shortly.

The Tzfat Kabbalists studied Jewish texts and practice, constantly searching for ways to add purpose and meaning (over and above "because we are commanded to") to Jewish observances that might otherwise slide into mechanized and meaningless "following orders." They understood the relationship between God and humans as dynamic, envisioning a heavenly "upstairs" life that paralleled and was actually influenced by our intentions as well as our behavior "downstairs," on earth. By choosing to count the forty-nine days of the Omer as seven seven-day weeks, they found a structure to give form and understanding to some of their loftiest philosophical musings on God and our relationship with God, and to guide their followers to transform these musings from pure thought into actions and behaviors.

In recent years, people have been re-discovering the practice of counting the Omer as an opportunity for spiritual preparation for the Shavuot re-experience of revelation — an echo, in some way, of our ancestors' journey out of Egypt and through the desert to Sinai. This book is intended to encourage adults and children to walk this journey of exploration and inquiry together, in much the same way that our forebears journeyed young and old together, each with questions that they needed to ask and answer according to their ability to wonder and understand.

When kids see their parents paying attention to their own spiritual journey, they learn that this annual cyclical journey is a tool they can bring into adulthood

— that "figuring things out" is for adults too. It allows them a glimpse of Judaism as an organic process rather than as a static and unmovable monolith.

The work in this book is different from other exercises you may have encountered. There are no "right" answers. This levels the playing field, placing parent and child together on a path where they can ask each other resonant and important questions and where they can discover and share new insights.

Generally, the adult world does not give kids enough credit for their ability to work with ideas of personal spiritual process and progress. But when children learn the skill of engaging in this process while they are young, they can deeply, viscerally know that spiritual inquiry is not only permissible, but encouraged and necessary for growth. They can be empowered by their need for exploration as they mature, rather than feeling bereft as beliefs formed in childhood become frayed by the demands and pressures of a less-sheltered adolescence and adulthood. In helping them to develop a fluid and rich spiritual life when they are most receptive, we equip them well for the journey ahead. As they move out of the family home and into their own independence, they will view it as another — albeit big — step in the journey they have been traveling all along, and that the destination is growth - and more questions.

Current educational theory and practice show that students feel a greater sense of ownership and accomplishment when they are not only permitted, but even pushed to form their own questions and investigations, and that they will learn best through their search for answers. When parents and their children share a journey of moral and spiritual inquiry, the experience can be personally meaningful and an opportunity for deep bonding.

At the end of the book of Malachi, we read the prophecy of the Messianic age heralded by the coming of the prophet Elijah, who will "turn the hearts of the fathers to their children and the hearts of the children to their fathers." When children and their parents are able to turn to each other to ask questions, discuss and learn, they have the potential to change the world. It is an awesome goal, and an achievable first step. Let's jump in.

The Sefirot - an introduction

Every translation is an interpretation. There is no way to express in one language everything that a word from another language really means. Every time you try to share an experience or story with another person, even in the same language, it is nearly impossible that the person listening will hear what you were really trying to say. It is even harder if you are trying to explain ideas that are ephemeral and laden with subtext, like kindness, goodness, balance or glory. These kinds of words mean different things to each of us; we 'interpret' them without even knowing that we are doing it.

The Hebrew word *sefirah* (*sefirot* is the plural) carries many ideas rolled into one word. *Sefer Yetzirah*, one of the key kabbalistic texts, explains it as follows:

> ... and He created His universe with three books (utterances),
> with text ספר,
> with number ספרה,
> and with communication (a story) סיפור.

In the phrase *Sefirat haOmer* its meaning is 'counting,' but the same root letters are at the heart of *sefer* – book, *l'saper* – to tell (a story), *safir* – sapphire and *sefirah* – a Divine emanation or aspect. It is this last which provides the Rabbis with a starting point for their concept of sefirot as a means of trying to get closer to God through understanding aspects of the Divine "personality," and finding those same characteristics within ourselves.

The ultimate questions of "life, the universe and everything" suffer from being far too vast to comprehend. Kabbalah, the Jewish mystical tradition, developed the system of sefirot as a way of distilling and parsing their actions and feelings in order to be able to isolate and examine one particular aspect of questions about God and about our very existence, and then set that part aside for a time to be able to focus on a different aspect. It all ends up connected in the end, but we can really only envision it in parts. We do not have the capacity to hold the whole in our minds as a limitless whole.

The Kabbalists enumerate ten sefirot, emanations, that provide the connection between the Infinite, Unknowable God and our earthly reality. Sefer Yetzirah says: "Ten sephirot of nothingness, ten and not nine, ten and not eleven." Later Kabbalists divided them into two groups. One, closer to the Infinite, and more hidden from us, comprises the three sefirot of Chochmah, Binah, and

Da'at. (Their Hebrew acronym, Chabad, became the name of the Chabad chassidic movement.) The remaining seven are considered the "lower" sefirot. It is those seven sefirot that are the focus of our exercises in this book.

Simply setting aside the period of Sefirat haOmer as a time for reflection and self-examination leaves the task far too vague for there to be any real progress and growth. With seven weeks of seven days, the cycle of Sefirat haOmer lends itself handily to a framework for self-examination as follows: Each week is assigned a sefirah, and each day within that week is also assigned a sefirah. So, within each week, we examine one particular way of expressing the sefirah of the week by thinking about the way that the two sefirot intersect. For example, the first week is assigned to be the week of Hesed. The first day of each week is also assigned Hesed. So, on the first day of the Omer we will look at the Hesed that is found within and expressed through the greater theme of Hesed. On the second day, we will move on to considering the expression of Gevurah within the theme of Hesed, and so on for the first seven days of the Omer. On the eighth day, or the first day of the second week, we will return to the expression of Hesed, but this time it will be through the framework of Gevurah, the sefirah assigned to the second week.

What follows is my best interpretation (though by no means the only interpretation) of the English translations of the sefirot as they are applied to one's concept of God and to the divine mechanisms at work in the cosmos and on earth. We can use these ideas as a tool, a lens through which to examine ourselves and our interactions.

There are usually two sides to every action: how it is intended and how it is received. When you have a misunderstanding with someone over something one of you said or did, it was probably because of the difference between what one thought they were doing and what the other understood or felt about it. The description of the sefirot in this book will address both; how we understand each to be an aspect of God, and how we can look at each one and work on that part of the way we behave. In order to be clear and consistent within the pages of this book, I will use the word 'attribute' and 'emanation' to refer to ways in which we experience the Divine (Divine attributes), and 'characteristic' or 'trait' to describe an aspect of our individual personalities.

Please take great care!! The questions we ask and things that are considered through this work are intended as a path to understanding ourselves and learning to do better things in the world - they are not intended to be used to tell someone else how they are 'doing it wrong.' In the realm of spiritual growth, each of us is responsible for how we, ourselves, will progress. I suspect that this was the real reason that the early mystical thinkers wanted to limit the study of these kinds of questions about God, humans and the workings of the universe to those who fit a certain profile. It is difficult but essential to separate your internal spiritual life from your experience of and interactions with those around you. Please try to hold in your head and heart simultaneously your belief in what is right and true along with an authentic and deep respect for the beliefs of others and the ways in which they behave. One of the greatest values for anyone studying this path is to be aware of and care for the feelings of other people. Self-righteousness has no place in this journey; always recognize that others may have different paths and different maps, entire inner lives hidden from everyone but themselves. **Be gentle with yourself and others.**

Introducing the Sefirot

חֶסֶד **Hesed** – Lovingkindness, Mercy. The original kabbalistic idea of Hesed as an emanation of God is the never-ending kindness that God shows us, whether or not we are deserving. (Many Christians understand this as 'grace.') Hesed is not based on our particular merit. It is simply a gift, given freely to all in the same way that the sun shines for everyone — not only for those people who are especially deserving of a sunny day. In the transposition of understanding from 'attribute of God' to 'human characteristic,' Hesed becomes our ability to be kind and gracious to everyone, regardless of social standing, intelligence, material goods or even looks. Hesed emerges from how we try to connect with others in whatever way we can. It is the characteristic of Hesed that encourages us to reach out to others in times of crisis, why we donate whatever we can when there has been a disaster, why bearing witness to cruelty and poverty can bring us to tears.

גְּבוּרָה **Gevurah** – Strength, Judgment, Discipline. Possibly the greatest manifestation of God's attribute of Gevurah can be seen in the thing people are most critical of: God does not interfere. There is tremendous Divine restraint in the lives of humans; we have been given free will, and are able to behave as well or as badly as our conscience dictates. One of the deepest mysteries of our experience of the Divine in our lives is that we really don't know what counts as Hesed and what counts as Gevurah until some time after the events have passed. Something that felt like Divine punishment in the moment can turn out to have led to the greatest opportunity in our lives.

It is useful to remember that we are commanded to bless the good and the bad equally* because we cannot truly know which is which in the moment, and ultimately it all comes from the same source**. When we turn this lens inward, we must examine ourselves for how quick we might be to rush into judgment or scorn of another person. It is not our place to judge the behavior of others; we cannot know the whole story. The 'discipline' aspect of Gevurah also reminds us to balance our impulse for Hesed, which is easy to give and feels good, with the discipline of Gevurah. We need to be heroic in holding the line, though it is difficult at times, as we navigate around temptations and find our 'true north.' We need to consciously and consistently examine our own motives and actions even as we discipline ourselves to refrain from being harsh with others. Gevurah is usually associated with God's left hand, balancing out Hesed which is associated with the right, making Hesed just a little stronger — assuming God is right handed!

תִּפְאֶרֶת **Tiferet** – Balance, Beauty. As an attribute of the Divine, Tiferet is the perfect balance of Hesed and Gevurah, the elegant solution to the seemingly unsolvable problem. Tiferet is delicate; difficult to perceive, easy to lose sight of. As a human trait, it is that ability to be both kind and firm at the same time; to be approachable by others while confident in our own unknowable soul.

A visual metaphor: Tiferet is the very fine beauty of a work of art, with the Gevurah influences giving form to the shape and discipline to the strokes and artistry, while Hesed influences the color, texture and light, bringing the work to life. As we dash through a busy, hectic day, Tiferet is the ability to realize and appreciate a fleeting instant of perfection when we see it and feel it. Take a moment to stop, watch, breathe, and savor it close to your heart, even if you then must rush on.

נֶצַח **Netzach** – Victory, Endurance. The victory of Netzach is not a brief moment of success, but truly overcoming something huge and seemingly insurmountable. Not just a win, but a triumph. As an attribute of God, we understand Netzach to be God's eternal and indestructible existence. God existed before anything else did and will continue to exist past the end of time. Understanding Netzach as a characteristic within ourselves is a little more challenging: What is it within ourselves that is our most basic, most real self?

---

[6] Talmud Bavli Berachot 54a
[7] Mishna Berachot 9:5

Who are we really, after we stop acting to impress other people (or ourselves)? The Netzach part of us is the spiritual backbone that enables us to survive a really bad day and still get out of bed the next day. It is the part within ourselves that is eternal, essential and unchanging — that by which we might define ourselves, if asked "What are you?"

הוֹד **Hod** – Splendor, Glory. Where Tiferet is beauty found in a delicate balance of things external to us, Hod is powerful inherent glory, the kind of beauty which has nothing to do with looks and everything to do with presence. As an emanation of God, we can see or experience Hod in the welling up of feeling we may have on witnessing small miracles or on becoming entranced with aspects of the natural world. When our pagan ancestors felt the urge to worship various parts of the natural world, they were probably responding to the insistent pull of Hod. If you pay attention, you can see this quality of deep and essential beauty in some people you know. You feel better just being around them, and they walk so beautifully through the world. Each of us has that potential inside us, and the challenge of examining the facets of Hod within ourselves is to recognize our own innate beauty, accept it and allow it to shine out in ways that can make the world a better place.

יְסוֹד **Yesod** – Foundation, Grounding. Yesod is the culmination and combination of all of the previous sefirot into that which is essentially and foundationally you. It is the meeting of the Divine and the experiential within you. Though the word suffers from overuse, Yesod within you is your soul, your connection between the ineffable and the real world with all of its flaws and mess. Each person's foundation, soul, provides a basis for acknowledging God to be both an element of everything, and also completely untouchable and unknowable. From a human perspective, it is our ability to put our ideals into actions. In this context, Yesod is the source of how we behave, who we show ourselves to be when we are in the real world behaving in real time. The measure of the human characteristic of Yesod is found in how closely your beliefs and goals align with the actual choices you make each day. The Divine emanation of Yesod is seen in all of the ways that things equalize and find stasis. The aspect of Yesod allows us to move through our days with confidence and courage.

מַלְכוּת **Malchut** – Sovereignty, Majesty. Malchut is the holy place of connection between you and the world, the roots of the Divine planted firmly in the real world. It is recognizable in our faith in foundational constants about ourselves and about the workings of the world in which we live. Malchut is the place where our core needs to interact with others, to react and integrate all that happens and still behave in ways that are true to our own deepest, truest soul/self. We live in the physical world with all of its complexity and all of the other souls who are our fellow travelers. Malchut is our connection to the past, the future and all that is possible. As an attribute of God, this is quite simply God's ultimate existence outside of and beyond human conceptions of time and being. It is a level of being that is at once so eternal and so imperceptible that the only way to "get it" is to take it on faith. All of the other sefirot lead us to this one, the Malchut of humanity; the Malchut of the Divine.

Malchut is what is being referenced in the concluding line of the Aleinu prayer when we pray for a day when God will be one and God's name will be unified. This does not mean that everyone will suddenly practice the same religion. Rather it means that humans will understand that relating to God, or Higher Power, as each one understands it, while acknowledging their fellow travelers' ability to make that connection through different practices and beliefs is the greatest possible expression of God's ultimate sovereignty, Malchut. In the human realm, we have to accept the essential Malchut of others in our interactions with them, no matter how boorish, mean or insignificant they may seem to us and no matter how difficult this may seem. Harder still is the mandate to recognize our own inherent Malchut, that is, our individual right to exist and the responsibility that goes with it.

Sometimes it can feel as though our presence on the planet is not very significant in the greater scheme of things. The characteristic of Malchut reminds us that not only do we have a right to be here, but a responsibility to make the best possible use of whatever it is we have been given to do. Just as we may not always recognize the face of Hesed or Gevurah when we see it, we cannot know the impact we have on others. Our essential Malchut is that part of our being which is elemental force and influence. Each of us has the ability to behave graciously or hatefully, kindly or horribly. When we hold in our minds the idea of our characteristic of Malchut we should also be mindful of the ways in which we use it.

Logistical notes for visualizations:

The best approach to practicing the visualization exercises in this book is to have one member of the family, group or class read aloud at a relaxed pace, giving the others plenty of time come to their own places and understandings.

If you are alone, read through the visualization a few times so that you have somewhat memorized the internal "map" of the path. Then close your eyes, spend a little time centering yourself and leaving the outside world outside. Take yourself through the visualization as you remember it. When you have finished — and it does not matter if you followed the exact path or followed through these ideas on a path of your own — it may be useful to write down some notes on the page about your experience. Perhaps you will come across these notes next year and continue to explore.

Counting the Omer – The Basics

The Omer is counted in the evening after true dark, usually about 45 minutes after sundown. We customarily take care not to mention which day of the Omer we will count before we do so ritually. If someone needs clarification of which day will be recited after the blessing, we mention that "yesterday was…", as a way of avoiding inadvertently "counting" before it ritually counts.

Here is the format for the recitation of counting:

בָּרוּךְ אַתָּה יְיָ אֱלֹהֵינוּ מֶלֶךְ הָעוֹלָם אֲשֶׁר קִדְּשָׁנוּ בְּמִצְוֹתָיו וְצִוָּנוּ עַל סְפִירַת הָעֹמֶר.

Blessed are You, Adonai Eloheinu, Ruler of the universe, who has sanctified us with Your mitzvot and commanded us to count the omer.

Baruch Atah Adonai, Eloheinu Melech ha-olam, asher kid'shanu bemitzvotav, vetzivanu al sefirat ha-omer.

There are a number of written kavanot (intentions) that some people add in order to enhance their concentration and focus. You may choose one or more to be a regular part of your counting ritual, or you may choose to vary them in order to make the practice of Sefirat HaOmer most meaningful to you. We havce included a selection in the Appendix.

Week 1 – The Week of Hesed

It is not what to do, but how much love we put into the doing. We cannot do great things, only small things with great love.

— Mother Teresa

Throughout the week of Hesed, we will come to see that Hesed connotes a deeper and more complex idea that the mere translation "kindness" communicates. It means kindness freely expressed, "just because." Hesed might be considered "senseless kindness" given without consideration of whether or not the recipient "deserves" it, something that goes far beyond just being nice.

The week of Hesed is also the week of the Pesach holiday itself. The combination of celebrating the holiday and the scent of spring in the air may encourage us to be more open to new spiritual approaches. It is the perfect time to explore this new path to find different ways to seek out and express the traits of Godliness within ourselves. No doubt, we will also identify qualities within ourselves that do not serve God or ourselves. The two-fold nature of this journey will be to uncover the holy sparks which we may not have noticed or appreciated in our lives while also letting go of old ways of thinking or being, without getting stuck in our regret about how we have acted in the past.

Our journey begins with Hesed, reminding us to treat not just others, but also ourselves kindly and gently. We are all-too ready to criticize ourselves or to hear criticism when we enter into a process of evaluation and introspection. Too often, this becomes so painful that we quickly abandon our efforts.

After the experience of the seders where we relive the exodus from Egypt, we continue our journey forward out of the slavery of feeling stuck in our old ways of being into the freedom to change. When we start with Hesed, we are beginning with one of the hardest parts; remembering to be kind to ourselves even as we are working to change old habits of mind and body which feel so inextricably bound up in the self we are.

It might seem surprising that we begin with the more heavenly Sefirot and work our way "down" into the concrete world. It makes sense, at first glance, to "get our house in order" in a physical and behavioral sense before tinkering with our spiritual way of walking in the world. However, the first week of the Omer takes place during the week of Passover, when our physical surroundings have been upended, the food we eat is different and everything seems new and a little strange. Not only do we experience a difference in our eating habits, but in some households we live with a complete 'kitchen makeover.' A lot of the things that we do on Passover are the same from year to year even as they are different from our usual day to day habits. During the preparation for the holiday, as well as at the seder itself, there is a good chance we have rediscovered treasures and heard melodies and tales that are familiar and yet encountered with a new understanding. The preparation and the memories stirred up by thoughts of previous years gives the holiday a duality of sameness/difference as we think about where we have been, spiritually, physically and emotionally, and what will be the same or different as we move forward in the coming year.

As we progress through the weeks of the Omer cycle, the questions we will explore will affect not only our ways of thinking, but hopefully our behavior as well. The goal is to be mindful about our lives as we actually live them in the day-to-day choices we make. The changes to which we aspire will find more fertile soil in a soul that has first been turned over and given extra air and ideas to breathe. Over the course of the seven-week journey from Passover to Shavuot, we hope to grind away some of our rougher edges, and find ways to buff up our finer traits. We will work our way from the sublime to the practical and real-world, and in the process, we hope that we will find ways of bringing a new awareness of holiness into our ordinary lives.

In Jewish tradition, we make frequent reference to Gemilut Hasadim", acts of lovingkindness, by which we mean, things we do without expectation of remuneration or personal gain, human expressions of unconditional caring. This would be Hesed in its purest form. Because we are human, we very rarely, if ever, feel or do something for only one purpose or motivation; we seem to have been deliberately designed to have mixed feelings. As you progress through this week and the ones to follow, try to attune yourself to the mix, rather than trying to box any experience into just one label. Look for the nexus of connection between the attributes for each day and see what happens when our inspirations and inclinations collide in the laboratory of real life.

Today is one day of the Omer הַיּוֹם יוֹם אֶחָד לָעֹמֶר

Kindness within Kindness חֶסֶד שֶׁבְּחֶסֶד
Hesed be-Hesed

When I was young, I admired clever people.
Now that I am old, I admire kind people.

— Abraham Joshua Heschel

Tonight is the second night of Passover. Many Jews have a second seder, and will recite the song Dayyenu, a long list of all of the separate actions which culminated in our release from slavery and our formation as a nation. Each one is counted as a separate act of Hesed from God. When we take the time to consider the many steps it took to bring us from slavery to freedom, we create space for awe and wonder, a space in which to fully appreciate just how amazing it is that we are here today.

Attention to detail can help us to become more aware of the many choices we make in our own lives that can result in either a kind or unkind outcome. There are many moments in the course of an ordinary day when we can choose to be kind, indifferent or mean. Perhaps a smile and 'thank you' to the driver of the bus as you are getting out at your stop, perhaps an extra moment to help a classmate or colleague gather their thoughts or collect their belongings. Maybe even just offering to do the dishes in an evening when it would be very appreciated. How will you choose to take your kind intentions and turn them into kind actions?

Share with Others:

Think of a time when someone did for you an act of pure kindness, and how that made you feel. Try to find at least one small way today to be kind for no better reason than that you thought of it.

WEEK 1 - HESED

Today is two days of the Omer

הַיוֹם שְׁנֵי יָמִים לָעֹמֶר

Strength within Kindness
Gevurah be-Hesed

גְּבוּרָה שֶׁבְּחֶסֶד

Tenderness and kindness are not signs of weakness and despair, but manifestations of strength and resolution.

— Khalil Gibran

Kindness is often perceived as an easy thing to offer, if only we were more inclined toward it. But sometimes, the strength in kindness is to be found in holding yourself back from rushing to help; allowing the one you care for to achieve or fall on their own, knowing you care, and feeling comfortable that you will *not* rush in to take over when things get tough. Good friends can be most supportive when they express confidence in each other's abilities, helping by assuring one another that they will be there supportively, no matter what. The Gevurah in Hesed says, "I know you can do it," or, "Let's do it together," rather than, "Here, let me do it for you."

Self-Reflection:
What is the hardest thing for you about Hesed? Do you think it takes more strength to help or not to help? Can you think of a time when someone helped you by stepping back rather than rushing in?

Today is three days of the Omer　　　　הַיּוֹם שְׁלֹשָׁה יָמִים לָעֹמֶר

Beauty within Kindness　　　　תִּפְאֶרֶת שֶׁבְּחֶסֶד
Tiferet be-Hesed

Practice random kindness and senseless acts of beauty.

— Anne Herbert

Tiferet — beauty and balance — is the ideal blend of Hesed and Gevurah. The word also conveys a sense of adornment; beauty that is outside of the usual experience. Tiferet b'Hesed is finding the beautiful inside the kindness. The graceful in the grace. We each have different notions of deep beauty, and it is usually not physical beauty that Tiferet is describing. Witnessing an act of unusual kindness, hearing a haunting melody or simply recognizing yourself in the words of something you read and being changed by the experience: all of these can be experiences of Tiferet.

In the Bible, Hannah pours her heart out to God in a prayer to conceive a child. She moves her lips, but makes no sound and Eli, the priest who observes her jumps to the conclusion that she is drunk. When she explains the situation, we can feel his harsh attitude change, and he wishes her well. In that moment of reframed understanding lays the balance and beauty of Tiferet she'beHesed. As Eli shifts his stance from condemnation to conciliation, his Hesed shines out because of the change in him through the aspect of Tiferet.

Brainstorm Together:
Is there an area in your family life where you might be less judgmental and more accepting? What would be the first step in making that change?

Today is four days of the Omer הַיּוֹם אַרְבָּעָה יָמִים לָעֹמֶר

Victory within Kindness נֶצַח שֶׁבְּחֶסֶד
Netzach be-Hesed

But remember, boy, that a kind act can sometimes be as powerful as a sword.

— Rick Riordan

The victory of Netzach beHesed is a victory by gentle means rather than brute force. The characters in the very popular books by Rick Riordan demonstrate these traits. They win by being kind, clever and open to unusual ideas. There are times when in order to be triumphant you have to find a new approach, something completely unexpected. The combination of Netzach and Hesed brings the understanding that grace can be experienced or shared in unusual ways. Something that seemed impossibly difficult can sometimes be turned around into an opportunity for unexpected growth and good.

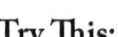

Try This:

As you go through your day, look for an event, a story, a picture or experience to share tonight in which you found kindness, creativity and ultimately triumph. You can write about it or print and place the picture here:

Today is five days of the Omer

הַיּוֹם חֲמִשָּׁה יָמִים לָעֹמֶר

Glory within Kindness
Hod be-Hesed

הוֹד שֶׁבְּחֶסֶד

My religion consists of a humble admiration of the illimitable superior spirit who reveals himself in the slight details we are able to perceive with our frail and feeble mind.

— Albert Einstein

Many people see Divine Glory in the ever-changing beauty of nature as well as its constancy: a setting sun is gloriously beautiful rather than terrifying because we know that it will rise again on the other side of the night; the order and arrangement of the stars in that night sky amaze us with their beauty, and also provide a reliable and ordered set of signs for navigation.

Though he lived through incredibly turbulent times in which unspeakable horrors happened, Albert Einstein, not a particularly religious man, nonetheless is remembered for his comment "God does not play dice with the universe." It was this faith that there had to be an organizing foundation, and a sincere belief that it could be found, which must certainly have made it possible for him to continue to pursue his own ultimately successful path of observation, discovery and calculation, long after most people had given up on him.

Go Out and Learn:

Take some time today and tonight to go outside. Notice some of the details in the changing environment of spring. Are there trees just starting to bud, small shoots of flowers beginning to show? You might want to choose a particular tree or area to observe weekly over these seven weeks and watch the effect of the passage of time from early spring into almost-summer.

Today is six days of the Omer　　　　　　　　　הַיוֹם שִׁשָׁה יָמִים לָעֹמֶר

Foundation within Kindness　　　　　　　　　יְסוֹד שֶׁבְּחֶסֶד
Yesod be-Hesed

No act of kindness, no matter how small, is ever wasted.

— Aesop

Finding the grounding, the foundation, of Hesed is the work of the everyday. It is relatively easy, and certainly much more gratifying, to do something big and flashy and generous — something others will definitely notice. It is far more difficult to be unfailingly polite, no matter how irritating the situation, or to remember to acknowledge those who do the little things that make your day go more smoothly.

It is a show of great kindness (as well as patience) to slow down for someone who is having a hard time keeping up, and to go at their pace for a while. The Yesod in Hesed is found in the everyday routine, and the small kindnesses to others. Sometimes it might be as small a gesture as a smile and thank-you to the bus driver, or reaching down to pick up something. As we get into the habit of performing such small kindnesses, we might become, while never knowing it, the best thing that happened for someone else in any given day.

In Your Life:
This evening, sit with whoever shares this book with you and tell them about the small things they do that you appreciate more than you mention. Try to become more aware of the ways that your small actions and choices can mean a lot to others. These do not have to be spiritual or religious: you can unroll your socks before putting them in the laundry; a parent or caregiver might put something extra and fun into a child's lunch bag. These everyday kindnesses show an ongoing awareness that the little things you do affect others.

**Today is seven days,
making one week of the Omer**

הַיוֹם שִׁבְעָה יָמִים
שֶׁהֵם שָׁבוּעַ אֶחָד לָעֹמֶר

Majesty within Kindness
Malchut be-Hesed

מַלְכוּת שֶׁבְּחֶסֶד

The first peace, which is the most important, is that which comes within the souls of people when they realize their relationship, their oneness with the universe and all its powers, and when they realize at the center of the universe dwells the Great Spirit, and that its center is really everywhere, it is within each of us.

—Black Elk

As the cycle of the week concludes we find our most human selves in Malchut, majesty. It is almost impossible to behave with true Hesed toward others until we experience Hesed within ourselves. Awareness of ourselves as being the one in charge of how we choose to be allows us to see that same "self-ness" in others, and to respect it rather than ruin it. You are not made any better by belittling someone else; in fact, your reduce yourself in their eyes, in your own esteem and in the eyes of anyone who witnessed it.

When we conjure an image of an historical Native American, someone like Chief Black Elk, our image is likely to be of someone who walked in harmony with the land and did not seek the destruction of others. While this ideal might be more mythology than history, it gives us something to aspire to, as all good myths do. When we find the "Great Spirit" inside of ourselves, then walking in Hesed becomes a natural thing to do.

Self-Reflection:
What do you think your best personal quality is? How do you allow that to shine for others? (This is how you would find your own Malchut she'be-Hesed) What characteristics do you seek out in your friends?

Continued on next page

Visualization: Malchut be-Hesed

This exercise can be a good relaxation before bed or in a quiet space when you need to remind yourself of where your center is. Feel free to return to it as often as you wish.

In the quiet time before falling asleep tonight, re-read the quote from Black Elk. Visualize yourself walking comfortably and naturally through a forest. Listen for the wind in the trees and the rustlings and chirps of all of the living creatures. After you have spent a little time there, see if you can identify what some of your greatest strengths are. These are core characteristics that are always present inside yourself. Imagine yourself writing them in some way. Read the words you have written and see them as a permanent piece of who you are.

As you end your visualization, return from the quiet place of nature to your own living reality, carrying the certain knowledge of your strength like a note that you have written to remind yourself of something important.

If you know what your strengths are, it can be a resource you draw from as you face situations where you might be tempted to be less than your best self. See this strength as a tangible thing that you can actually reach out and touch in your mind's eye.

You may wish to write some notes and thoughts about your strengths. It can be helpful to remind yourself of the experience.

Week 2 – The Week of Gevurah

Eight is the number of infinity,
one more than what you know how to be...

— Matisyahu

As we begin the second week of the Omer with the eighth day, the rhythm of our nightly recitation changes because we add the numbering of weeks to the number of days. As we shift focus from the sefira of Hesed to the sefira of Gevurah, the eighth day starts a week of looking at all of the facets of strength — strength expressed as well as the strength required to hold back from expressing. There are times in our lives when the strongest thing we may have to do is to do nothing and let events take their natural course. Gevurah comes from the same root as "gibbur," hero. This week we'll consider that heroism comes in all shapes and sizes. There will be times when you do or say something that doesn't seem very big or important, and yet this very action may be the thing that makes it possible for someone else to experience enough Gevurah that it changes their life.

The eighth day is significant in a few different contexts in Judaism. For baby boys, the bris happens on the eighth day; Hannukah lasts for eight days; and we transition out of Passover at about this time as well (some Jews observe Passover for seven days and some for eight). Perhaps the most powerful "eighth day" would be the day after God completed the creation of the world. Every possibility was open — the entire universe had been created and now it was up to the humans to carry on with the work of creation, picking up where God left off. In some ways, perhaps we live in an eternal "eighth day."

This week, we will bring Gevurah more clearly into focus, so that we are conscious of both expressing it and experiencing it. In some primal way, we are like the first humans, finding the strength to keep our focus and commitment to counting the Omer as we slip from the holiday time back into our regular lives and habits. You may not realize just how strong you are until you watch your self in action this week and think about the different ways that true strength can be expressed.

**Today is eight days,
making one week and one day
of the Omer**

הַיּוֹם שְׁמוֹנָה יָמִים
שֶׁהֵם שָׁבוּעַ אֶחָד
וְיוֹם אֶחָד לָעֹמֶר

Kindness within Strength
Hesed be-Gevurah

חֶסֶד שֶׁבִּגְבוּרָה

*Nothing is so strong as gentleness,
nothing so gentle as real strength.*

—Saint Francis de Sales

Tonight, with the end of Passover, as we make the transition back into our 'normal lives,' we can think about the strength and the kindness that are required in order to truly be free. Someone who is genuinely strong has no real need to enforce their will in harsh ways, even if, at times, they must exercise their power. There is strength in offering help, and there is courage in accepting it.

When we looked at Gevurah be-Hesed, we considered how there could be strength in kindness through choosing the times to give and the times to hold back. When we look at the aspect of Hesed be-Gevurah, we can consider the times when the greatest kindness might be to step in, step up, take charge — not to hold back. A friend or family member might need someone else to help them by being the responsible one for a while, even if this is very hard to ask for. The hardest part of Hesed be-Gevurah is knowing when to take bold action and when you can be supportive without taking over. Each of these ways of supporting someone is useful in its proper context. Understanding that you have a choice in how you support someone by reflecting on the meaning of Hesed be-Gevurah may provide a framework and a guide for your actions.

Tikkun Olam:

What if you saw someone being bullied at school *(for grown-ups, perhaps a co-worker who is having a hard time at work)*? You would like to help, but you also know that doing something noticeable might only make their situation worse. How could you help this person in a way that reflects the value of Hesed be-Gevurah? How might you act if the person was someone you didn't like very much?

**Today is nine days,
making one week and two days
of the Omer**

הַיּוֹם תִּשְׁעָה יָמִים
שֶׁהֵם שָׁבוּעַ אֶחָד
וּשְׁנֵי יָמִים לָעֹמֶר

Strength within Strength
Gevurah be-Gevurah

גְּבוּרָה שֶׁבִּגְבוּרָה

Strength does not come from winning. Your struggles develop your strengths. When you go through hardships and decide not to surrender, that is strength.

—Arnold Schwarzenegger

Our greatest struggles are with our own selves: our habits of thought and action. It is far easier to push your physical body to the limit in one extreme moment than it is to quit a bad habit and to choose each day not to return to it. There is a saying that 'when you are stuck in your own head, you are caught behind enemy lines.' In other words, sometimes we ourselves are our own worst obstacles to achieving our goals and dreams. We can also be very hard on ourselves, getting upset over every small flaw we think we see in ourselves, when how and who we are is actually completely fine. In this context, Gevurah be-Gevurah is the ability to be strong enough to let our positive strength show and not to be the first one in line to beat ourselves up. When we live in Gevurah be-Gevurah, we use our power to hold our internal harsh critic back in order to let our unique and true strength shine.

Try This:

As you go through the next few days, try to catch yourself in the act of putting yourself down or minimizing your accomplishments. Notice when this happens, or if it happens.

Make some notes so you can share these experiences later in the week.

**Today is ten days,
making one week and three days
of the Omer**

Beauty within Strength
Tiferet be-Gevurah

הַיּוֹם עֲשָׂרָה יָמִים
שֶׁהֵם שָׁבוּעַ אֶחָד
וּשְׁלֹשָׁה יָמִים לָעֹמֶר

תִּפְאֶרֶת שֶׁבִּגְבוּרָה

It is time for parents to teach young people early on that in diversity there is beauty and there is strength.

—Maya Angelou

Tiferet describes beauty and balance. Tiferet can be a physical balance of beauty, strength and discipline, an elegant solution to a puzzle or a particularly striking work of art. Tiferet is mostly in the eye and heart of the one seeking it. The hardest kind of Tiferet to describe is how you can find beauty and balance in the strength within yourself.

In the case of expressing your opinions, too much focus on discipline can lead to a very harsh and unforgiving approach. You might be intolerant of other people's feelings without meaning to be. It is important to recall the aspect of Tiferet be-Gevurah as you share your thoughts and opinions, so that you can be very clear that you are expressing your own feelings, and that you understand and respect that others may think and feel differently. The art of expressing yourself in a way that is clear and true to yourself while also being gentle and respectful of others is a fine balance of Tiferet be-Gevurah — keeping true to your beliefs, while taking care that others are also heard and respected.

Brainstorm Together - Putting thoughts into action:

Choose a topic to practice with at home (or in class). At first express your thoughts about it in the most absolute terms, as if it were clearly black and white, without leaving any allowance that you might accept that anyone else could feel differently.

After you have listened to how these statements sound spoken aloud, brainstorm together ways you can change how you share your opinion so that it is still the same opinion, yet acknowledges that others may think or feel differently. By practicing in a safe space, you can hear how the different modes of expression feel to the listener. The next step is to reach for your new understanding when you find yourself in a challenging conversation.

**Today is eleven days,
making one week and four days
of the Omer**

הַיּוֹם אַחַד עָשָׂר יוֹם
שֶׁהֵם שָׁבוּעַ אֶחָד
וְאַרְבָּעָה יָמִים לָעֹמֶר

Victory within Strength
Netzach be-Gevurah

נֵצַח שֶׁבִּגְבוּרָה

*Our greatest weakness lies in giving up.
The most certain way to succeed is always to try
just one more time.*

—Thomas A. Edison

Netzach is the expression of creative victory. Thomas Edison did not succeed in his first, second or even third try. He had an idea, and he kept on trying until he somehow made it work. Plenty of people have great, creative ideas all of the time, but too often, they give up when their idea does not work quickly or easily. The characteristic of Netzach be-Gevurah is in continuing to work toward something even when you are discouraged and you feel like you will not succeed. You may need to try a new approach, or talk it over with someone, or walk away for a little while to clear your head and then have the Gevurah to return to the challenge. The victory is in the persistence.

In Real Life:
What task, tough situation or conversation have you been avoiding? When you think about it, what is getting in the way of making a start? Can you picture what it will look like and how you will feel when you succeed?

Sometimes it is difficult to begin a project or start to do a chore, and it is very tempting to push it off and find something else to do. It seems to be human nature to avoid work unless there is some powerful incentive or motivation. Sometimes, being able to envision the end result can provide the motivation we need to get to work and make progress toward the goal. When we have a very clear picture of the result and the satisfaction it will bring, it becomes much easier to get to work on the "dreaded task."

Continued on next page

Visualization: Netzach be-Gevurah

Think of something you have been avoiding, or just something that you know you need to do, but have not started yet. Spend some time sitting quietly and try to picture what it will look like when it is finished, how you will feel, the sense of accomplishment when you have completed this task. Picture yourself doing the things that will get the job done, remembering what it is going to look like and feel like when you are finished.

Spend some time with this, until you can call it to mind easily, filling in details and embellishing. Now you are ready to start; you can see the beauty that your effort will create. When you are tempted to push it off, use all of the Gevurah you can muster to call on the images and feelings from your visualization to help make getting the task done a pleasant, positive action rather than a draggy, disagreeable chore.

Make some notes to encourage yourself and to help you remain mindful of the positive outcome your work will have.

Today is twelve days, making one week and five days of the Omer

Glory within Strength
Hod be-Gevurah

הַיּוֹם שְׁנֵים עָשָׂר יוֹם
שֶׁהֵם שָׁבוּעַ אֶחָד וַחֲמִשָּׁה
יָמִים לָעֹמֶר

הוֹד שֶׁבִּגְבוּרָה

I don't think of all the misery but of the beauty that still remains.
—Anne Frank

Hod is frequently translated as glory. "Glory" can seem like too grand a word for our ordinary lives. After all, we are just going along from day to day. Where is the glory in that? But if we seek out beauty and reach out to others, that action can be strong and glorious and beautiful.

Anne Frank was a young girl, just twelve years old, during the terrible events of World War II that we call the Shoah or Holocaust. She kept a diary which her father found after she had been killed. He published it so the world would know the reality of daily life during that terrible time. Her thoughts, concerns and feelings are mostly the usual issues of a girl growing up. Reading her words while knowing the trials her family suffered can give you a new perspective about your own life. No matter how awful your situation there is beauty to be found, which might shine all the more brightly and be that much more precious because of how dark and desperate the world around you is. Don't be shy about reaching for glory.

Sharing Tonight:

A few nights ago, the 'to do' for the day was to watch yourself in action and see if you allowed your full strength to shine. Tonight is a good night to share your experiences and to consider them, not only through the lens of Gevurah be-Gevurah, but also through the lens of Hod be-Gevurah. In what ways do your strengths bring glory to yourself and to those whose lives you touch?

Unfortunately, there are many parts of the world where darkness and horror are a fact of many kids' lives, even today. Spend some time thinking and talking about ways that you can ease another child's situation and bring a little more strength and beauty into his or her life.

Yom HaShoah ve HaGevurah usually occurs on the 27th of Nisan, corresponding to the 12th day of the Omer

Today is thirteen days, making one week and six days of the Omer

הַיּוֹם שְׁלֹשָׁה עָשָׂר יוֹם
שֶׁהֵם שָׁבוּעַ אֶחָד וְשִׁשָּׁה
יָמִים לָעֹמֶר

Foundation within Strength
Yesod be-Gevurah

יְסוֹד שֶׁבִּגְבוּרָה

Being deeply loved by someone gives you strength, while loving someone deeply gives you courage.

—Lao Tzu

Yesod, Foundation, Love. It is truly amazing what courage and strength we can find within ourselves when it is for the well-being of someone we deeply love. Parents might want to take the opportunity tonight to tell their child(ren) the story of one time they had to dig down and find the courage to do something for them. It might be something as trite as going on the roller coaster and pretending not to be scared, or something as truly heroic as leaping into action in a dangerous situation in order to ensure their child's safety. Kids can imagine the ways that the love of their family and close friends might give them the strength to make it through a tough day, (and kids do have tough days, just like grown-ups).

Words into Actions:

Foundation **Love** **Strength** **Yesod** יְסוֹד

Spend some time with these words, think about how they work in your life.

Write them on cards or slips of paper and carry them with you for the day tomorrow. When you think of it take one out and see if the word pulled from your pocket fits in with what is happening at that moment. Did it help you to notice something that you hadn't seen before? Make some notes on the card or paper to share tomorrow night.

**Today is fourteen days,
making two weeks of the Omer**

הַיוֹם אַרְבָּעָה עָשָׂר יוֹם
שֶׁהֵם שְׁנֵי שָׁבוּעוֹת לָעֹמֶר

Majesty within Strength
Malchut Be-Gevurah

מַלְכוּת שֶׁבִּגְבוּרָה

*I believe you have to be better
than you ever thought you could be.*

—Ken Venturi

As the cycle of the week concludes, we return to Malchut, Majesty. There is a superficial and obvious connection between Majesty and Strength, but the purpose of our journey is to try to see past the obvious. In many modern film-fairy tales, the true hero turns out to be someone unexpected. They may or may not be the one with the high position (prince, princess or otherwise), but they are the one who has shown unexpected strength and persistence in the face of obstacles. Perhaps this is true majesty, finding strength when you did not know you had it, and finding majesty within your strength.

Bringing It Back Home:

Share last night's cards and thoughts tonight, and then spend some time with these questions:

Has the work of this week changed how you see yourself as a strong person?

How do you think you can help others to see their own Gevurah?

Do you believe it is easier to encourage other people or to encourage yourself?

WEEK 2 - GEVURAH

Week 3 – The Week of Tiferet

*For the honey and the thorn, for the bitter and the sweet,
for our sons and daughters — dear God, keep them safe.*

—Naomi Shemer

In the third week of the Omer, we will examine the aspects and characteristics of Tiferet: beauty/balance. We began by looking at Hesed, exploring ways of being kind and seeing kindness in the world around us. This past week we focused on Gevurah, strength in all of the ways it can be experienced and expressed. Tiferet, the balance between these two aspects of how we feel and act, is more subtle, and will require finely tuned attention to observe it within ourselves and to find ways to nurture its growth in our lives.

Additionally, the modern Israeli holidays of Yom Hazikaron and Yom Ha'atzmaut occur during this week. These two special days, celebrated as a connected whole, show one kind of balance in our lives — the balance between tragedy and celebration.

Yom Hazikaron is the Israeli parallel to Memorial Day in America, and Yom Ha'atzmaut is the parallel to the Fourth of July. But there is a huge difference in the tone of observance of these holidays. In contrast to the American use of Memorial and Independence Days for shopping, trips to the beach and barbeques, Israel continues to have meaningful memorials for its fallen and celebrations of its continued existence. Yom Hazikaron is widely observed by Israelis as a day of memory and mourning for fallen soldiers. When the day of heartache ends at nightfall, the joy and celebration of Yom Ha'atzmaut begins. The connection between the two days helps each to be observed with a sharper attention to its meaning.

Celebrating the anniversary of Israeli independence feels much more than "happy" when we have the mourning of Yom Hazikaron fresh in our minds. The juxtaposition helps people to make the connection between the sadness and sacrifices that soldiers and others made and make every day, for the sake of the State of Israel and the fact that despite more struggle and controversy than any other nation in the world, Israel remains a sovereign, democratic state. Because of this intentional connection, it is unlikely that Israelis will ever lose sight of the focus of these days.

This week, we will be looking for all of the places in our lives where we can find beauty and balance. We will also be celebrating these two very important days.

Today is the fifteenth day, making two weeks and one day of the Omer

Kindness within Beauty
Hesed be-Tiferet

הַיוֹם חֲמִשָּׁה עָשָׂר יוֹם
שֶׁהֵם שְׁנֵי שָׁבוּעוֹת
וְיוֹם אֶחָד לָעֹמֶר

חֶסֶד שֶׁבְּתִפְאֶרֶת

For beautiful eyes, look for the good in others;
for beautiful lips, speak only words of kindness;
and for poise, walk with the knowledge that you are never alone.

—Audrey Hepburn

Audrey Hepburn was a beautiful, famous British actress. Besides just being famous and beautiful, she acted to help when she thought something was wrong or unfair. Ms. Hepburn was a child in Europe during World War II, both experiencing and witnessing a terrible amount of hunger and suffering.

As an adult she saw that children in Ethiopia and other poorer countries were as hungry as people had been during the war. She worked tirelessly to help make things better. This is truly Hesed, seeing someone else's pain and trying to help in the best ways possible. She could have ignored the hard truth, but instead she used her public presence to urge others to join her in her work. She embodied Hesed be-Tiferet, a kindness in beauty that helped to make the world aware, and probably saved many lives.

Judaism teaches us that true beauty is in the balance of your heart, in your ability to act with both strength and kindness.

Treasure Hunt:
The quote at the top of the page is one description of what it might mean to live Tiferet. Write the quote on an index card and carry it with you through the next few days. See if you notice at least one example of each piece of the quote:

1) a time you noticed someone behaving in a particularly good way when they could have just as easily chosen otherwise;

2) a time when you could have said something nasty or sassy, but you chose words of kindness instead;

3) a time when the knowledge that you are not alone, that you have the love and support of friends and family helped you to get through a tough moment.

WEEK 3 - TIFERET

Today is the sixteenth day, making two weeks and two days of the Omer

Strength within Beauty
Gevurah be-Tiferet

הַיּוֹם שִׁשָּׁה עָשָׂר יוֹם
שֶׁהֵם שְׁנֵי שָׁבוּעוֹת
וּשְׁנֵי יָמִים לָעֹמֶר

גְּבוּרָה שֶׁבְּתִפְאֶרֶת

A mode of conduct, a standard of courage, discipline, fortitude and integrity can do a great deal to make a woman beautiful.

—Jacqueline Bisset

Most people think of a sunset or a flower when they hear the word beauty. Your first reaction to the word is likely to be about beauty beauty you can see. Now that you have gained new perspective on beauty as Tiferet, balance between kindness and strength, you may be open to thinking of other ways of being beautiful besides just being pretty. Gevurah be-Tiferet allows us to focus on the strength in beauty. There can be an invisible beauty in a level of strength that is above and beyond anything you think you can do.

Jacqueline Bisset is a British actress who began her career in roles that featured her physical beauty as well as her acting ability. With the passage of time, she was able to find roles that were centered more in a depth of character, and not just in looking young and pretty. She says that she finds these roles more interesting and more enjoyable because she is in a position to cause her audience to think more.

Words into Actions:

Courage   **Discipline**   **Fortitude**   **Integrity**

If you had to pick one, and only one of these, which do you think is the most important?

Is there a person or event that comes to mind when you think of this word?

Today is the seventeenth day, making two weeks and three days of the Omer

Beauty within Beauty
Tiferet be-Tiferet

הַיּוֹם שִׁבְעָה עָשָׂר יוֹם
שֶׁהֵם שְׁנֵי שָׁבוּעוֹת
וּשְׁלֹשָׁה יָמִים לָעֹמֶר

תִּפְאֶרֶת שֶׁבְּתִפְאֶרֶת

Beauty is not caused. It is.

—Emily Dickinson

Tiferet is a blend and balance of strength and kindness. This is already a difficult balance to work for. To find the perfect beautiful balance within that perfect balance is probably not something that can be forced by a lot of hard trying. As the poet Emily Dickinson states so simply, it is. There are some things that happen because you relax and allow them to happen instead of working to cause them to happen. These moments are precious because you can not create them; you can only be aware enough to notice and appreciate them when they happen.

Have you ever seen something so amazing that it took your breath away? Chances are, you were able to witness it, but you could not have made it happen.

Take a Walk:

On this journey from Pesach to Shavuot, we have explored and will continue to look at many 'things-of-the-mind'. We have looked a lot at how we behave, with others and with ourselves. Now it is time to get outside!

By now, we are well into spring. Spend some time appreciating the changes that are happening in the physical world around you. The weather is warmer, the days are longer, the leaves are growing, and you may even be seeing the start of flowers. The world is coming into bloom after a time of stillness. "Beauty is not caused. It is." Go out and see it. Try to be attentive to the things you may never see again.

The world is amazing and filled with wonders. It is worth taking the time to notice and appreciate it.

Today is the eighteenth day, making two weeks and four days of the Omer

Victory within Beauty
Netzach be-Tiferet

הַיּוֹם שְׁמוֹנָה עָשָׂר יוֹם
שֶׁהֵם שְׁנֵי שָׁבוּעוֹת
וְאַרְבָּעָה יָמִים לָעֹמֶר

נֶצַח שֶׁבְּתִפְאֶרֶת

If you will it, it is no dream.

—Theodore Herzl

Netzach be-Tiferet – for those who find meanings in various numbers, today, the eighteenth day, is special because the Hebrew notation for eighteen also spells chai, the Hebrew word for life. To comemorate the two modern Israeli holidays celebrated this week, we honor the lives of some heroic people who worked so hard to make the dream of a Jewish homeland into the reality of the State of Israel. One of these people, Theodore Herzl, penned the famous and inspirational words above in 1902 with respect to the creation of a Jewish homeland. The same sentiment can be applied to any large goal that we pursue despite many pressures and obstacles. Netzach be-Tiferet, heroism within beauty, may indeed be the thing that inspires people to work for their dreams, even when it seems that the dream is impossible.

A Time to Reflect:

Tonight, we catch up a bit, taking some time to reflect on and share about some of what we noticed and did in the past few days.

Share and try to draw some connections from the Treasure Hunt exercise at the start of the week and your mindful walk yesterday.

Today is the nineteenth day, making two weeks and five days of the Omer

הַיּוֹם תִּשְׁעָה עָשָׂר יוֹם
שֶׁהֵם שְׁנֵי שָׁבוּעוֹת
וַחֲמִשָּׁה יָמִים לָעֹמֶר

Glory within Beauty
Hod be-Tiferet

הוֹד שֶׁבְּתִפְאֶרֶת

*I do not bring forgiveness with me, nor forgetfulness.
The only ones who can forgive are dead;
the living have no right to forget.*

—Chaim Herzog

Today is the primary date on the calendar for Yom Hazikaron, though it is sometimes adjusted when a conflict with Shabbat arises. On this day just before Yom Ha'atzmaut, people who live in Israel are reminded, with sirens and moments of national silence, of the sacrifice that was and is being made in order for the State to come into existence and continue to thrive. Imagine what it is like when an entire country stops at the same moment and quietly reflects. We bring the power of silence to this day because no words are adequate. What a powerful force is silence.

Hod is frequently translated as glory, but glory can seem like too grand a word for our day-to-day lives. After all, we are just going along, doing our routine activities, living from day to day. But what if we did consider glory as a part of our ordinary lives? What if, in some way, the little things we do become glorious, simply because we made good choices in those moments?

In this context, imagine the exquisite glory and honor present and expressed in the moments of silent remembrance in the streets of Israel.

Go and Learn:
Spend some time today in quiet reflection about the State of Israel and all that it means to you...

Then, learn one new way in which Israel is important in a positive way. Start to prepare to celebrate Yom Ha'atzmaut tomorrow with Israeli decorations and foods, music and art by Israeli artists, or any other way in which you would like to honor the existence of the State of Israel.

WEEK 3 - TIFERET

Today is the twentieth day, making two weeks and six days of the Omer

Foundation within Beauty
Yesod be-Tiferet

הַיּוֹם עֶשְׂרִים יוֹם
שֶׁהֵם שְׁנֵי שָׁבוּעוֹת וְשִׁשָּׁה
יָמִים לָעֹמֶר

יְסוֹד שֶׁבְּתִפְאֶרֶת

Today, in most years, if celebrations would not interfere with Shabbat observance, is Yom Ha'atzmaut. It seems like a perfect fit with the day of foundation within beauty/balance. Israel is such a basic, foundational piece of our Jewish identity.

Many people have never seen or read the Declaration of the Establishment of the State of Israel. It is worth reading and thinking about. Do you think modern Israel represents the intention of its Declaration? Is there anything in this document that surprises you? Spend some time together reflecting on this.

Declaration of the Establishment of the State of Israel
(Translation)

> ERETZ-ISRAEL was the birthplace of the Jewish people. Here their spiritual, religious and political identity was shaped. Here they first attained to statehood, created cultural values of national and universal significance and gave to the world the eternal Book of Books.
>
> After being forcibly exiled from their land, the people kept faith with it throughout their Dispersion and never ceased to pray and hope for their return to it and for the restoration in it of their political freedom.
>
> In the year 5657 (1897), at the summons of the spiritual father of the Jewish State, Theodore Herzl, the First Zionist Congress convened and proclaimed the right of the Jewish people to national rebirth in its own country.
>
> This right was recognized in the Balfour Declaration of the 2nd November, 1917, and re-affirmed in the Mandate of the League of Nations which, in particular, gave international sanction to the historic connection between the Jewish people and Eretz-Israel and to the right of the Jewish people to rebuild its National Home.

The catastrophe which recently befell the Jewish people — the massacre of millions of Jews in Europe — was another clear demonstration of the urgency of solving the problem of its homelessness by re-establishing in Eretz-Israel the Jewish State, which would open the gates of the homeland wide to every Jew and confer upon the Jewish people the status of a fully privileged member of the comity of nations.

Survivors of the Nazi holocaust in Europe, as well as Jews from other parts of the world, continued to migrate to Eretz-Israel, undaunted by difficulties, restrictions and dangers, and never ceased to assert their right to a life of dignity, freedom and honest toil in their national homeland.

In the Second World War, the Jewish community of this country contributed its full share to the struggle of the freedom- and peace-loving nations against the forces of Nazi wickedness and, by the blood of its soldiers and its war effort, gained the right to be reckoned among the peoples who founded the United Nations.

On the 29th November, 1947, the United Nations General Assembly passed a resolution calling for the establishment of a Jewish State in Eretz-Israel; the General Assembly required the inhabitants of Eretz-Israel to take such steps as were necessary on their part for the implementation of that resolution. This recognition by the United Nations of the right of the Jewish people to establish their State is irrevocable.

This right is the natural right of the Jewish people to be masters of their own fate, like all other nations, in their own sovereign State.

Accordingly we, members of the People's Council, representatives of the Jewish community of Eretz-Israel and of the Zionist movement, are here assembled on the day of the termination of the British mandate over Eretz-Israel and, by virtue of our natural and historic right and on the strength of the resolution of the United Nations General Assembly, hereby declare the establishment of a Jewish state in Eretz-Israel, to be known as the State of Israel.

We declare that, with effect from the moment of the termination of the Mandate being tonight, the eve of Sabbath, the 6th Iyar, 5708 (15th May, 1948), until the establishment of the elected, regular authorities of the State in accordance with the Constitution which shall be adopted by the Elected Constituent Assembly not later than the 1st October 1948, the People's Council shall act as a Provisional Council of State, and its executive organ, the People's Administration, shall be the Provisional Government of the Jewish State, to be called "Israel".

The State of Israel will be open for Jewish immigration and for the Ingathering of the Exiles; it will foster the development of the country for the benefit of all its inhabitants; it will be based on freedom, justice and peace as envisaged by the prophets of Israel; it will ensure complete equality of social and political rights to all its inhabitants irrespective of religion, race or sex; it will guarantee freedom of religion, conscience, language, education and culture; it will safeguard the Holy Places of all religions; and it will be faithful to the principles of the Charter of the United Nations.

The State of Israel is prepared to cooperate with the agencies and representatives of the United Nations in implementing the resolution of the General Assembly of the 29th November, 1947, and will take steps to bring about the economic union of the whole of Eretz-Israel.

We appeal to the United Nations to assist the Jewish people in the building-up of its State and to receive the State of Israel into the comity of nations.

We appeal — in the very midst of the onslaught launched against us now for months — to the Arab inhabitants of the State of Israel to preserve peace and participate in the upbuilding of the State on the basis of full and equal citizenship and due representation in all its provisional and permanent institutions.

We extend our hand to all neighbouring states and their peoples in an offer of peace and good neighbourliness, and appeal to them to establish bonds of cooperation and mutual help with the sovereign Jewish people settled in its own land. The State of Israel is prepared to do its share in a common effort for the advancement of the entire Middle East.

We appeal to the Jewish people throughout the Diaspora to rally round the Jews of Eretz-Israel in the tasks of immigration and upbuilding and to stand by them in the great struggle for the realization of the age-old dream - the redemption of Israel.

Placing our trust in the "Rock of Israel", we affix our signatures to this proclamation at this session of the Provisional Council of State, on the soil of the homeland, in the City of Tel-Aviv, on this Sabbath eve, the 5th day of Iyar, 5708 (14th May, 1948).

David Ben-Gurion

Today is the twenty-first day, making three weeks of the Omer

הַיּוֹם אֶחָד וְעֶשְׂרִים יוֹם שֶׁהֵם שְׁלֹשָׁה שָׁבוּעוֹת לָעֹמֶר

Foundation within Beauty
Yesod be-Tiferet

יְסוֹד שֶׁבְּנֶצַח

People are like stained-glass windows. They sparkle and shine when the sun is out, but when the darkness sets in, their true beauty is revealed only if there is a light from within.

—Elisabeth Kubler-Ross

As the cycle of another week concludes, we return to Malchut, majesty. Malchut be-Tiferet inspires us to do whatever is in our power to create the kind of beauty that Tiferet imbues through simple existence. Earth Day, in the United States, often falls sometime during this week, reminding us of the Tiferet in this beautiful planet that we inhabit without having done anything at all to merit it. We take for granted not only our very existence, but the fact that we exist in a beautiful place that supplies all that we need to provide for ourselves.

The aspect of Malchut is closely associated with the earth as a planet. When we do all we can to preserve the delicate balance that is the beauty of Tiferet, perhaps we are allowing the Malchut aspect of our soul to shine a little brighter.

Brainstorm Together:

What are some ways that we can minimize waste in our day-to-day lives?

Are there healthier choices we can make when we consider things like our food or water? How can we help to make the earth a better, healthier place than it is now?

One way to physically interact with the aspect of Malchut be-Tiferet is to bring a plant into your home, to care for and tend, and perhaps to benefit from. An aloe plant has many uses and is very easy to maintain. Basil is another popular plant. It is not as easy to maintain as aloe, but you can use the fresh basil leaves in all kinds of delicious foods.

WEEK 3 - TIFERET

Week 4 – The Week of Netzach

Good character is not formed in a week or a month.
It is created little by little, day by day.
Protracted and patient effort is needed to develop good character.

—Heraclitus

In the fourth week of the Omer, we focus on the aspect of Netzach: Victory/Endurance. This fourth week is also a sort of of nexus or tipping point between the first weeks of the Omer and the last. During the first weeks, the focus may be seen as increasing our holiness, or behaving in a more Godly way. The sefirot we focus on in the later weeks are more closely associated with the down-to-earth issues of daily living.

Though the aspect of Gevurah as strength may seem to be very similar to the understanding of Netzach, the two are subtly different. When we considered Gevurah, we looked at strength sometimes as restraint and sometimes as the choice to take powerful action — always demonstrated in immediate time. This week, with Netzach, we are looking at a kind of strength generally understood to be endurance and sometimes defined as triumph or victory: strength over extended time. Another way of considering it might be that you would call on Gevurah to help you resist an immediate temptation, while Netzach would represent the accumulated result of all of your Gevurah decisions.

This fourth week of the Omer, this middle week of the journey, with three weeks before and three weeks after, marks a turning point from ideas to behavior, from thinking to doing. There will always be a mix, but as we continue our count, we will continue step by step to grow closer to who we are at our core and how we want to act in the world.

Netzach is the kind of victory and strength that we show when we continue on with something, even when the going gets tough, even when we think we do not want to do it anymore. We can show our true Netzach colors when we persist and do not give up.

Today is the twenty-second day, making three weeks and one day of the Omer

Kindness within Victory
Hesed be-Netzach

הַיּוֹם שְׁנַיִם וְעֶשְׂרִים יוֹם
שֶׁהֵם שְׁלֹשָׁה שָׁבוּעוֹת
וְיוֹם אֶחָד לָעֹמֶר

חֶסֶד שֶׁבְּנֶצַח

An effort made for the happiness of others lifts us above ourselves.

—Lydia M. Child

Too often, people assume that in order to win, someone else needs to lose. And yet, the victories in our lives are so much sweeter if we know that others have also benefitted from our good fortune. The lesson of Hesed be-Netzach, the kindness within victory, is that when we help others on their path, very often our own lives are made better too.

Lydia Child was a 19th century woman who fought for what she believed. She fervently believed in the equality of all people: men and women, black, Native American, or white. Her views were not always popular; she was a woman ahead of her time. Much of the source of her Netzach was in the Hesed of her beliefs, and though she saw only minimal success, her writing and work cleared a path for those of us who followed.

In Your Life:

Very often, when we get into an argument with someone, we feel like we have to win, or else we will lose — that is, in order for me to come out okay, you have to be diminished in some way. But if we put some thought into it, maybe taking some time to let our tempers cool down a bit, there is usually a way for both of us to be satisfiedv. The secret is in trying to find a way for everyone to be on the side of solving the problem at hand. Instead of trying to win, think of what your real goal is and try to find out what the other person's real goal is too. This would truly be an act of Hesed be-Netzach.

WEEK 4 - NETZACH

Today is the twenty-third day, making three weeks and two days of the Omer

Strength within Victory
Gevurah be-Netzach

הַיּוֹם שְׁלֹשָׁה וְעֶשְׂרִים יוֹם שֶׁהֵם שְׁלֹשָׁה שָׁבוּעוֹת וּשְׁנֵי יָמִים לָעֹמֶר

גְּבוּרָה שֶׁבְּנֶצַח

For man, as for flower and beast and bird, the supreme triumph is to be most vividly, most perfectly alive.

—David Herbert Lawrence

There are days when life feels very thorny, when every action feels like a trial and nothing is easy. Everyone, whether adult or child, has days like this. Some people may have better ways to hide or cope with it than others, but for all of us, some days are just hard. Adults need to honor, rather than minimize, the experiences of those who are younger: the hurts are much more keenly felt by someone who has not yet had much experience in living with frustration and loss, triumph and victory. It is far more supportive to value and validate the feelings and experiences of each other — for young and old alike, as the song says, "Mama said there'd be days like this…"

So it is indeed both strength and triumph that brings you here. You have stuck with the process, continued on the journey through both challenges and easier times, and hopefully picked up some new appreciation and skills along the way. Today is a day for recognizing and relishing the strength it takes to be precisely you, without any pretense or posturing. You are created as you are: the goal of this journey is not only self-improvement, but also recognizing and valuing your inherent self-worth. Be 'most vividly, most perfectly alive' today.

Visualization: Gevurah be-Netzach

(It may be useful for one person to read this aloud while others close their eyes and focus their attention on the voice of the reader.)

Envision yourself in a secluded garden or a comfortable room where you are at peace, with no pressing concerns. Take some time to explore how it feels to be safe from criticism and free to exist in whatever way you wish. As you remain still, self-critical thoughts or "I should"s may begin to form, unbidden, in your mind. Gently push them away outside of your space. At this moment, the only thing you need to do is exist. Your presence here is the most important thing for those who love and care for you. It is all that is required of you in this moment — simply to feel that you, just being yourself, belong in the world.

After some time has passed, look around the space you have created behind closed eyes. What do you see? With what have you surrounded yourself? Is there a particular color in your "mind palace?" Are there things around you that have some meaning? Have you placed yourself in a real space you can identify and go to, or is this as-yet unexplored terrain? Take your time and look around.

After the exercise, write about what you saw and felt. It may take more than one attempt before you find the place that suits you, just you, but once you find it, it is a place to which you can return when you need to recharge and renew your spirit.

Today is the twenty-fourth day, making three weeks and three days of the Omer

הַיּוֹם אַרְבָּעָה וְעֶשְׂרִים יוֹם שֶׁהֵם שְׁלֹשָׁה שָׁבוּעוֹת וּשְׁלֹשָׁה יָמִים לָעֹמֶר

Beauty within Victory
Tiferet be-Netzach

תִּפְאֶרֶת שֶׁבְּנֶצַח

The best and most beautiful things in the world cannot be seen or even touched — they must be felt with the heart.

—Helen Keller

Where do we find the elusive beauty that is Tiferet? The sefirah of Netzach is symbolic of endurance and strength, and does not, on the surface, include such a delicate element as Tiferet. But the Netzach endurance of Tiferet can be found in the things we may not ordinarily notice or think much about.

Helen Keller experienced the world in a way that most of us cannot imagine. Deprived of sight and sound, she still sought out the company of others and enjoyed the sensations available to her. With all of our sensory power, and a huge amount of input to process, it can take a considerable amount of strength of mind for us to focus in on enjoying some basic pleasures. It might be worth a lot to develop this skill.

Pay Attention (mindfulness):
Our lives are very multi-media; we listen while we write while snacking; we do our homework while carrying on text conversations while watching TV. Rarely are we doing fewer than three things at once. Limiting yourself to one experience in a particular block of time can lead to an unparalleled enjoyment of the beauty of that thing. Practicing one-thing-at-a-time, even briefly, can win you a small victory over the enervating multitasking culture that has become the norm.

Today, spend a small period of time enjoying one activity or experience, with singular focus on every aspect of it that you can sense. For example, if you are listening to music, spend the time only listening to the music, hearing each note and each instrument; listen for the silences in between the notes. If you are eating an apple, focus on the apple and only eat the apple. Fully immerse yourself in the muscular jaw and throat movements, the taste, the crunchiness, the difference in texture between the peel and the flesh, and the resounding noise of each bite.

Jot down some thoughts about your focused, one-at-a-time experiences.

Today is the twenty-fifth day, making three weeks and four days of the Omer

הַיּוֹם חֲמִשָּׁה וְעֶשְׂרִים יוֹם שֶׁהֵם שְׁלֹשָׁה שָׁבוּעוֹת וְאַרְבָּעָה יָמִים לָעֹמֶר

Victory within Victory
Netzach be-Netzach

נֶצַח שֶׁבְּנֶצַח

We all have dreams. But in order to make dreams come into reality, it takes an awful lot of determination, dedication, self-discipline, and effort.

—Jesse Owens

Netzach within Netzach calls out to the very core of our will. Jesse Owens embodied all that it took to envision and then achieve success. Against political forces and social norms that, from the time he was young, told him that he would never be allowed much as a black man in America, he fought his way through and proved America and the entire world wrong. This does not mean he never had a doubt or was never tempted to give up, but rather that he persevered despite very great odds.

When Jesse Owens died on March 31, 1980, President Carter said of him, "Perhaps no athlete better symbolized the human struggle against tyranny, poverty and racial bigotry. His personal triumphs as a world-class athlete and record holder were the prelude to a career devoted to helping others."

Jesse saw his Olympic victories as a beginning, not the end of his work to help those around him. In this way, he is the embodiment of Netzach be-Netzach.

Time for Reflection:

Today is the middle day of the middle week, the half-way point in the Omer Journey: time to stop and take stock.

Have you been surprised by anything? Disappointed? Inspired? Look back over the time from Passover until now and think of all that has happened in your life. Write down the most significant details, things you might forget as they get swallowed up in the vastness of a passing year.

Give yourself credit for all that it took to reach this place in time, and renew your resolve to continue learning and growing.

Today is the twenty sixth day, making three weeks and five days of the Omer

Glory within Victory
Hod be-Netzach

הַיּוֹם שִׁשָּׁה וְעֶשְׂרִים יוֹם
שֶׁהֵם שְׁלֹשָׁה שָׁבוּעוֹת
וַחֲמִשָּׁה יָמִים לָעֹמֶר

הוֹד שֶׁבְּנֶצַח

Endurance is not just the ability to bear a hard thing, but to turn it into glory.

—William Barclay

The message of this week of Netzach is that each of us brings into the world an irreducible spark in the core of our being which cannot be snuffed out or removed by anything outside of ourselves. There are times when that spark may be hard to find, buried under layers of detritus from the outside world, but it is always there, whether or not we feel it in the moment.

The experience of Hod be-Netzach is the ability to walk around with the knowledge of that irreducible core, and to value ourselves because of it. Every one of us has some ways in which we shine, though they may not be measurable by external standards.

Try This:

If you had to distill your essence down to your core being, how would you describe it? That is, what is there about you that makes you essentially and uniquely you? Choose three things about yourself that you think are your very best qualities. How do these qualities help you when the going gets rough? Can you think of ways to strengthen these areas so that you become even better at handling difficult circumstances?

You may want to explore this in conversation with someone else — it sometimes can be hard to see our own best qualities. The insights of someone you trust can help you to see what you are too close to notice.

Today is the twenty-seventh day, making three weeks and six days of the Omer

Foundation within Victory
Yesod be-Netzach

הַיּוֹם שִׁבְעָה וְעֶשְׂרִים יוֹם שֶׁהֵם שְׁלֹשָׁה שָׁבוּעוֹת וְשִׁשָּׁה יָמִים לָעֹמֶר

יְסוֹד שֶׁבְּנֶצַח

Let there be many windows to your soul, that all the glory of the world may beautify it.

—Ella Wheeler Wilcox

There are times in our life when we may try very hard, only to be told that the work isn't good enough. At other times, a project may be judged 'excellent,' even when we know it was not our best effort. While it is tempting to allow outside sources to evaluate our efforts, it is far more reliable and honest to pay attention to our inner compass.

Yesod be-Netzach is the melding of our inner core of truth with the quality of our efforts and accomplishments. Of course, if something is not done well enough to satisfy external requirements, then it will need to be fixed, no matter how hard we believe we worked. But as a general rule, we should use our own Yesod-foundation of truth to honestly assess our efforts and evaluate the result. This means doing your very best work all of the time, even if you think you could get by with less. It is a very steep demand and a lifetime goal.

Bringing it Home:

As you go through your day today, try to catch yourself in moments when the inside evaluation and the outside assessment do not match. What are some of the circumstances? Is it about how hard you tried or how much work you put in? Is it simply a matter of opinion? Make a note of one or two situations and bring them to the table for discussion. How can you work to bring about a shift so that your inner core and the external world truthfully align?

Today is the twenty-eighth day, making four weeks of the Omer

הַיוֹם שְׁמוֹנָה וְעֶשְׂרִים יוֹם
שֶׁהֵם אַרְבָּעָה שָׁבוּעוֹת לָעֹמֶר

Majesty within Victory
Malchut be-Netzach

מַלְכוּת שֶׁבְּנֶצַח

Your present circumstances don't determine where you can go; they merely determine where you start.

—Nido Qubein

Malchut be-Netzach, the majesty, the Divine, within the victory of endurance. This is what we draw from within when we think we have given all that we can give, and we are called on to do just a little more. Like runners in a race, there are times when we 'hit the wall,' feeling that even one more step would be too hard. And yet somehow, when the situation is urgent, we can seemingly go beyond ourselves to summon up additional courage and strength that we did not know we had.

It is the quality of reaching beyond what we believe to be our limits that defines Malchut be-Netzach. Yesod finds us at our core, distilled being, while Malchut is what we can achieve when we reach beyond ourselves, pushing our endurance to a breaking point, and receiving a Divine assist when we must do what we thought to be impossible. As we conclude the week of Netzach and move forward into the week of Hod, glory, we can carry with us this open-ended idea of success in all areas of our lives.

The quote above reminds us not to be limited by what we think we can do, but instead to reach past what we think is possible for what we don't even yet know is possible. Mr. Qubein, a businessman, is no different than any one of us, except that he found that he had a way of helping people to find the best in themselves and to use all that they have available to achieve more than they thought they could.

Project:

Think of one area of your life you wish could be improved.

Can you think of any steps that are in your power to affect this area?

What would it take to make one small change?

Plan to use the week of Hod to take the step you need to start yourself on the road toward the change you are hoping to make.

Week 5 – The Week of Hod

Look out into the universe and contemplate the glory of God. Observe the stars, millions of them, twinkling in the night sky, all with a message of unity, part of the very nature of God.

—Sai Baba

In the fifth week of the Omer, we focus on the aspect of Hod, glory. This is a particular kind of glory, though. You cannot achieve it through external accomplishment or success. There is no amount of external honor that can bring about Hod. Rather, it is an indescribable quality of being illuminated from within when you engage in positive actions. If you have been with someone in whom you recognized some form of indescribable aura or glow — metaphorical or real — it was probably the internal glory, the radiating light of Hod.

How can you bring more Hod into your life, or set free the Hod that already resides within you? In terms of external action, Hod is found in community participation. Doing anything for the greater good of someone or something outside yourself can be a well-spring of Hod. Seeking out those people who make you want to be your best self can be another path toward greater realization of your inherent Hod.

In the course of this week, we will celebrate Lag baOmer, the 33rd day of the Omer. There is a great deal of lore and myth surrounding how this particular day came to be singled out as a day of joy amid the solemnity of this time of year. The most popular explanation is that in the first century of the common era, the students of Rabbi Akiva were dying from an illness that, legend has it, was brought on by their lack of respect for one another. On the 33rd day of the Omer, the plague miraculously abated. Whether it is legend or fact, the story carries a lesson for every day, not just the 33rd day of the Omer or even the period of Sefirat haOmer: Without respect for one another, anything else we do is diminished. If we wish to live a happy and healthy life, one of the central pieces is to live with a deep caring and respect for our fellow travelers.

Today is the twenty-ninth day, making four weeks and one day of the Omer

Kindness within Glory
Hesed be-Hod

הַיּוֹם תִּשְׁעָה וְעֶשְׂרִים יוֹם
שֶׁהֵם אַרְבָּעָה שָׁבוּעוֹת
וְיוֹם אֶחָד לָעֹמֶר

חֶסֶד שֶׁבְּהוֹד

As I've gotten older, I've had more of a tendency to look for people who live by kindness, tolerance, compassion, a gentler way of looking at things.

—Martin Scorsese

By now, we have been counting close to a month of days and exploring the ways in which we see and experience the world. As the quote from Martin Scorsese notes, the ways in which we understand things and the qualities we seek in our friends and in ourselves can evolve over time. A month is a relatively brief period of time when compared to your whole life, and yet it is also a long time when it comes to persisting in something and building a habit. If you have been counting every night, or even most nights, you might be surprised to realize that it has already become a habit.

Habits are actually easier to form than you think. If you make a commitment to form a habit and are rigorous with yourself about it, the reward will be wonderful. There is a tremendous feeling of pride in acquiring a new, positive habit. With luck the habit leads to a better self, which will serve to increase the Hod that radiates from within.

In Your Life:

Hesed — make it a habit! This is the fifth Hesed day we have counted. Hopefully, you now have an idea that habits can be formed (or lost) much faster than one would think. Identify a specific act of Hesed that you have been meaning to get into the habit of doing. Maybe you want to donate to a local soup kitchen, volunteer to help more at home, or shovel snow or rake leaves for an elderly neighbor. Make sure it is something that you could easily do and just as easily decide to neglect or postpone, "I'll do it tomorrow."

Continued on next page

Make a commitment to do it, think of why you want to do it, and write your plan and commitment down here, and then put that plan into action. You have the remaining days of the Omer period, and the rest of your life, to make it happen.

In counting the Omer, we have been living the idea that each day counts, that each day presents another chance to do something new. Add this specific act of Hesed to your life one day at a time and remind yourself each day why you believe it is important to stick by your commitment. Check back in the coming 'Hesed' days of the Omer to see how you are doing. If the goal needs to be changed, you can do that too, but do it with intention to find a way that you can bring your unique and beautiful Hesed to the world.

My plan to bring more Hesed into the world is:

Today is the thirtieth day, making four weeks and two days of the Omer

Strength within Glory
Gevurah be-Hod

הַיּוֹם שְׁלֹשִׁים יוֹם
שֶׁהֵם אַרְבָּעָה שָׁבוּעוֹת
וְיוֹם אֶחָד לָעֹמֶר

גְּבוּרָה שֶׁבְּהוֹד

Greatness lies, not in being strong, but in the right using of strength; and strength is not used rightly when it serves only to carry a man above his fellows for his own solitary glory. He is the greatest whose strength carries up the most hearts by the attraction of his own.

—Henry Ward Beecher

The greatest and most heroic form of glory, as noted in today's quote, is when something we do brings good not just to ourselves, but to those around us as well. Glory is a rather overused and poorly-understood concept: it is ultimately not about how great others think you are, but rather, it is about how good others feel when with you, and how much they can be inspired to achieve. There are plenty of small ways in which you can encourage those around you, even when you may have lost sight of the sparks of your own Hod.

Everybody has days on which they feel overwhelmed. On a day like that, it takes a lot of Gevurah, true heroism and strength, to get up, get out, and shine anyway. Do not measure yourself with someone else's ruler. You alone know how hard you worked to accomplish something. If you put a great deal of effort into something that seems small in your eyes, give yourself the full measure of appreciation for your accomplishment.

Family Roundtable:
Think about today's events. Choose something you did that seemed difficult or even impossible. If the day held no drama, you still were an active person today; and some things were easier than others. No matter how trivial, if there was a thing you did not want to do but you did it anyway,

Continued on next page

take that out and consider it. How did it feel to push beyond your comfort zone into a difficult place? Can you give yourself credit for the inner glory that shined through when you did?

   Share your stories with each other. Everyone, younger and older, has some actions and decisions that challenge them. The very thing that seems trivial to you may be much harder for someone else. In your family circle, honor the accomplishment of the person who acted, and help them to celebrate the Gevurah with which they acted today. Gevurah be-Hod is sometimes found in recognizing the greatness of the small triumphs of the people we live with and love, and in letting them know that their actions matter to you.

Today is the thirty-first day, making four weeks and three days of the Omer

הַיּוֹם אֶחָד וּשְׁלשִׁים יוֹם שֶׁהֵם אַרְבָּעָה שָׁבוּעוֹת וּשְׁלשָׁה יָמִים לָעֹמֶר

Beauty within Glory
Tiferet be-Hod

תִּפְאֶרֶת שֶׁבְּהוֹד

I believe that each of us comes from the Creator trailing wisps of glory.

—Maya Angelou

Maya Angelou, past poet laureate of the United States, expresses the vision of Tiferet be-Hesed beautifully in this simple phrase: "Wisps of Glory…" It so precisely captures the fleeting nature of the Hod we are examining this week. Not a big-fanfare, hero's glory, but rather a small though powerful Divine glory that is so difficult to see in others and perhaps even more difficult to recognize in ourselves.

The way that Angelou characterizes the Divine as "the Creator" with non-gendered language evokes an image of a Divine presence to whom we all — male and female, young and old — can relate. That we each are so different from one another, and each carry 'whisps of glory' can help us feel a little more agency and power as we go through the day.

Make Something Beautiful Today.

Make use of your inner creative spark to create, through photography, collage, poem, painting, or any other materials you wish, artwork that speaks to you of Tiferet be-Hod. Ephemeral beauty is so difficult to capture in ordinary words, and may be better expressed through art. Give yourself a little time and space with this idea; if you have not finished by the end of the day, do not worry. Keep at it until you have finished. Do not allow yourself to be frozen into inaction — start something even if you are not sure where it will lead. Give yourself license to have plenty of false starts. You can experiment and "mess around," you don't have to get it 'right' in any one attempt. Leave yourself open to the possibility of a later inspiration changing how you see Tiferet be-Hod. When you have created your work, you may choose to share it, or you may decide it is too personal to share.

Today is the thirty-second day, making four weeks and four days of the Omer

Victory within Glory
Netzach be-Hod

הַיּוֹם שְׁנַיִם וּשְׁלֹשִׁים יוֹם
שֶׁהֵם אַרְבָּעָה שָׁבוּעוֹת
וְאַרְבָּעָה יָמִים לָעֹמֶר

נֶצַח שֶׁבְּהוֹד

Not in achievement, but in endurance, of the human soul, does it show its divine grandeur and its alliance with the infinite.

—Edwin Hubbel Chapin

Netzach be-Hod, in its simplest translation would be the Victory in Glory. A surface glance makes this seem simple; after all, is that not exactly what glory is all about — victory? Dig a little deeper though, and a more profound idea emerges. No one particular triumph helps us to connect to our Hod, the inner glory that is hardest for us to see in ourselves. Rather, it is the endurance, the ability to hold to our principles, even when the temptation to take an easier way is strong, that helps us to see our internal Divine spark. One single act is a good start, but it is in our Netzach, our endurance and ability to keep that spark burning, that allows the Hod, the glory of being human, with all of the choices and dilemmas that entails, to shine.

Guided Visualization and Journaling:

Read the following, and then follow the script in your head to the best of your ability. Place writing materials within close reach so that you can capture what you thought and felt without needing to get up and move around too much.

Sit quietly. Close your eyes, allowing them to adjust to the darker space this places you in. Keeping your eyes closed, look around. You are looking within yourself. What you seek is your internal Divine spark. Where does it live within you? Do your best to keep away from outside ideas and to only travel inside of your own heart — this is very private. You pass through rooms filled with art, rooms filled with people you love, spaces that are open to the elements, with trees and sun and sky. In all of your known experience, where is that light shining for you?

When you have located something that feels like it shines and illuminates you, go to it and investigate more closely. Try to know everything you can about this spark that helps you to endure. When you feel you know what you need to know and you think you can keep the thoughts long enough to write them out, slowly return to the world of external reality and spend time writing about your experience.

You may want to try this a few times, or even to make it a regular practice. The first time, you might feel embarrassed and refuse yourself permission to get too close to that which is at your core. If so, write about that experience; Why do you think you felt embarrassed? How can you overcome that feeling so that you can come to know yourself better?

We tend to spend our lives doing what others expect of us, so it can be hard to venture into the realm of the thoughts about who we more deeply are and what we really want. The ability to locate and express our deepest wishes, even if they seem impossible, is true Netzach be-Hod.

Take some time to make some notes:

Today is the thiry-third day, making four weeks and five days of the Omer

Glory within Glory
Hod be-Hod

הַיּוֹם שְׁלֹשָׁה וּשְׁלֹשִׁים יוֹם
שֶׁהֵם אַרְבָּעָה שָׁבוּעוֹת
וַחֲמִשָּׁה יָמִים לָעֹמֶר

הוֹד שֶׁבְּהוֹד

A legend about Rabbi Akiva: He was asked, "Which is the more beautiful—God's work or man's?" Rabbi Akiva responded, "Undoubtedly man's work is the better, for while nature, at God's command, supplies us only with the raw material, human skill enables us to use these materials to create infinitely, according to the requirements of art and good taste." His Roman questioner had intended to trap Akiva, asking "Why has God not made man just as He wanted him to be?", (with respect to the ritual of circumcision), but Akiva responded calmly, "Because it is the duty of man to perform mitzvoth and improve himself"

This eye-opening conversation beautifully demonstrates today's combination of Hod be-Hod. Here we have Rabbi Akiva, one of the greatest figures in Jewish tradition, declaring that the human ability to create using the materials God has provided trumps God's ability to make the raw material available for humans to create with. It is hard to imagine this legendary sage taking such a seemingly modern view. Yet Akiva's view also encapsulates Hod be-Hod. Each of us is born with a spark of the Divine (Hod). Only through the remarkable power of human intent, imagination and ingenuity can we transform the spark into Hod be-Hod, the burning spirit within us. Even then, we have the power to choose to share the warmth and glow of that flame with others or to hide it.

Today, we celebrate Lag baOmer. The 33rd day of the Omer is closely associated with Rabbi Akiva and his students. Some legends tell of their courageous efforts to keep the study of the Jewish tradition alive under a repressive Roman regime. Other, less heroic tales reveal ways in which Akiva's students did not behave according to the teachings they were learning. Famously, many were killed by a plague, punishment attrbuted to this behavior. Might it be that somehow it was the behavior itself that killed them? With all of the stories and lore, it is thanks to Rabbi Akiva and his students who survived that we have the tradition as it is handed down.

Another legend regarding Rabbi Akiva places Moses at the back of Akiva's classroom, listening to him teach, and not recognizing a thing he says. In closing his lesson, Akiva is asked where the law comes from, and responds that it was brought down by Moses from Mount Sinai, at which point Moses turns to ask God how this is possible. God answers (more or less), 'because this is the way I have set it up.' The lesson here is that while we have received an ancient tradition, it is a living tradition, and it is up to us to put it into a context that makes sense to us, and to live, as Akiva did, according to our own best understanding of what is expected.

Lag baOmer is a great day for celebration, yet, as with everything in Judaism, it is a mixed joy. In remembering Rabbi Akiva and his students, we also remember the high price many of our ancestors paid for their Jewish observance through the ages. Though Jewish practice and observance is much easier for most of us now, we should consider it no less precious than Rabbi Akiva did.

Today is the thirty-fourth day, making four weeks and six days of the Omer

Foundation within Glory
Yesod be-Hod

הַיּוֹם אַרְבָּעָה וּשְׁלֹשִׁים יוֹם
שֶׁהֵם אַרְבָּעָה שָׁבוּעוֹת
וְשִׁשָּׁה יָמִים לָעֹמֶר

יְסוֹד שֶׁבְּהוֹד

*'Age' is the acceptance of a term of years.
But 'Maturity' is the glory of years.*

—Martha Graham

Martha Graham was a revolutionary dancer and choreographer. She has been compared to such greats as Picasso and Stravinsky, among others. After a full career, she retired in her early 70s, but it did not go well. She resumed her choreographic and teaching work, understanding that without expressing that essential part of her, she could not thrive.

A friend of Ms. Graham recalls a time when she was feeling uncertain about her own choreographic work. She recalls that Martha encouraged her, saying "There is a vitality, a life force, an energy, a quickening that is translated through you into action, and because there is only one of you in all of time, this expression is unique. And if you block it, it will never exist through any other medium and it will be lost. The world will not have it. It is not your business to determine how good it is nor how valuable nor how it compares with other expressions. It is your business to keep it yours clearly and directly, to keep the channel open. You do not even have to believe in yourself or your work. You have to keep yourself open and aware to the urges that motivate you."

"Keep the channel open..." Yesod be-Hod can be expressed in this way as well: keep the channel open, that is, find what is foundational for you, then do all you can to remove obstacles and clear the way for your best Hod, glory, to flow outward.

In Your Life:

What are you so passionate about that, if it wasn't part of your life, you would be less of yourself than you are? Acknowledge that passion now

— be it a creative energy, an analytical drive, a geeky-fandom, a sense of humor, or any other trait that is strong within you — and let yourself feel how it is a pathway to sharing yourself with the world.

The words that Martha Graham shared reminded her friend that she was uniquely able to contribute what she did. The same is true for each of us. In terms of the greater scheme of things, it does not matter if you think that someone else can do what you want to do better, the absolute fact is that no one else can do it precisely the way you will. So, make sure that you make time in your day to that which you wish to do. Do not wait for permission, because you already have it: There is only one of you in all of time. Be the most you, the Hod be-Yesod you, for all the world to see.

Today is the thirty-fifth day, making five weeks of the Omer

הַיּוֹם חֲמִשָּׁה וּשְׁלֹשִׁים יוֹם שֶׁהֵם חֲמִשָּׁה שָׁבוּעוֹת לָעֹמֶר

Majesty within Glory
Malchut be-Hod

מַלְכוּת שֶׁבְּהוֹד

Our greatest glory consists not in never falling, but in rising every time we fall.

—Oliver Goldsmith

In the immortal words of Big Bird, "Everyone makes mistakes, so why can't you?" Our lives are filled with mistakes, misjudgments, and moments when we wish the earth would open up to let us disappear from view. We dread these, and yet, they provide our greatest opportunities for growth. The process of growing can make us anxious, take us "out of our comfort zone." By definition, these experiences are uncomfortable. Yet, growth makes us stronger and better equipped to handle future uncomfortable situations. This is in some way the essence of Malchut. This final sefirah of Malchut is the one that is the closest to real life. Remember that every cycle begins with Hesed, a place of comfort, aspiration and very Godly ideas. Each week/sefirah proceeds from there, with each successive step bringing us closer to exploring how we bring our Divine-spark selves into the real, external, world in which we were placed by the same Divine hand that lit the unique spark within each of us.

We will fall sometimes — the system is designed that way. It is when we lift ourselves back up again and use the knowledge gained from the fall that we exemplify Malchut be-Hod, true majesty in glory.

Family Talk:
Spend some time considering the quote at the top of this day's page. When you think of the ideas of falling and rising, what situations come to mind? How can finding glory in trying again help you persevere in the issues you face in your own life?

Week 6 – The Week of Yesod

Your time is limited, so don't waste it living someone else's life. Don't let the noise of others' opinions drown out your own inner voice. And, most important, have the courage to follow your heart and intuition.

—Steve Jobs

Yesod as Foundation isn't just the idea of having something deep within you that is uniquely yours and that defines you. Yesod is also the ability to keep the integrity of that core, to be able to listen to your own voice and hear it more clearly than the voices of those around you. Only you can bring to the planet the unique gifts and insights that you have.

Yesod is located in the very center of our being, the place where the ideas and ideals of the past five weeks come to rest, grow and mix with other input, providing the inspiration and motivation for our conscious actions. Yesod is our core integrity — recognizing our own essence and then remaining true to that inner self.

The ultimate goal of the Sefira journey every year is to develop a greater awareness of our ability to choose to become more authentically ourselves, to choose to continue to grow emotionally and spiritually. Each year, as we count through the cycles of the days and weeks of the Omer, we work at finding our best human selves in preparation for re-experiencing the revelation at Sinai on Shavuot. Each year we hope to grow just that much more in our ability to understand our tradition and how each one of us will live it and experience it.

Today is the thirty-sixth day, making five weeks and one day of the Omer

Kindness within Foundation
Hesed be-Yesod

הַיּוֹם שִׁשָּׁה וּשְׁלֹשִׁים יוֹם שֶׁהֵם חֲמִשָּׁה שָׁבוּעוֹת וְיוֹם אֶחָד לָעֹמֶר

חֶסֶד שֶׁבִּיסוֹד

We ought to do good to others as simply as a horse runs, or a bee makes honey, or a vine bears grapes season after season without thinking of the grapes it has borne.

—Marcus Aurelius

Marcus Aurelius was a Roman emperor who lived at approximately the time the Mishna was finding its final form (during the second century of the common era). By most accounts, his personal behavior was completely in keeping with his position as Emperor. As the historian Herodian admires, "He gave proof of his learning not by mere words or knowledge of philosophical doctrines but by his blameless character and temperate way of life."

His advice here is much easier to say than to follow; we are each too prone to keeping score. Often, without thinking about it, we carefully weigh the way someone has behaved toward us in the same moment that we decide how to treat them. In the spirit of Hesed be-Yesod, finding the kindness that is embedded in your foundation, Aurelius' words ring true: aspire to be kind by nature. It is an ideal to reach for, to be able to do good as easily as any natural act, without planning or prejudice. This is one of those goals we are likely to return to a number of times in the course of our life, hopefully getting a little closer each time we aim.

Hesed Check-in:

Last week, we looked at Hesed be-Hod, the kindness inherent in the glory of our lives. You made a plan for how you would like to open yourself up and bring more Hesed into your everyday life. Today is the day to check in about that, especially as we seek to make kindness a more natural response within ourselves.

How has your greater awareness of Hesed in your life made a difference for you? What have you done to express Hesed and to accept Hesed from others? What improvements can you make?

Today is the thirty-seventh day, making five weeks and two days of the Omer

Strength within Foundation
Gevurah be-Yesod

הַיּוֹם שִׁבְעָה וּשְׁלֹשִׁים יוֹם שֶׁהֵם חֲמִשָּׁה שָׁבוּעוֹת וּשְׁנֵי יָמִים לָעֹמֶר

גְּבוּרָה שֶׁבִּיְסוֹד

The most common way people give up their power is by thinking they don't have any.

—Alice Walker

Your foundational power is your internal strength, your knowledge of what is right and wrong and your moral compass. In the combination of aspects of this day, the 37th day of the Omer, Gevurah be-Yesod, you can find the hero-strength that lies at the core of who you are. When you were born, you had as much power and as much right to use it as any other human being. It does not matter whether you were born rich or poor, in the United States or in a far less privileged country. When something or someone tries to push you into behaving in a way that is not true to your best and truest self, and it feels wrong at your core, you have the power to choose to accept or reject their view of you. Stand your ground and hold on to who you know yourself to be. It is this power that you give away when you let someone else's influence overrule what you know to be right. It takes Gevurah to recognize that power inside yourself and to treasure and hold on to it.

Share with Others:

Think of a time when you went along with what others were doing, or did something they told you to do even though it did not feel right. Can you locate in yourself the part of you that was trying to tell you it felt wrong?

Imagine yourself back in that same situation; can you imagine a way to have done things differently? Revisiting and rehearsing a re-do of such scenes, you can prepare yourself for the next time you find yourself in a tug-of war between your insides (how you know you want to be) and your outsides (what others are pushing you to do). You can strengthen your Gevurah muscles, just like you strengthen your arms and legs, through exercise and practice.

Today is the thirty-eighth day, making five weeks and three days of the Omer

Beauty within Foundation
Tiferet be-Yesod

הַיּוֹם שְׁמוֹנָה וּשְׁלֹשִׁים יוֹם שֶׁהֵם חֲמִשָּׁה שָׁבוּעוֹת וּשְׁלֹשָׁה יָמִים לָעֹמֶר

תִּפְאֶרֶת שֶׁבִּיסוֹד

A man who as a physical being is always turned toward the outside, thinking that his happiness lies outside him, finally turns inward and discovers that the source is within him.

—Søren Kierkegaard

This week of Yesod is all about looking into yourself to notice and strengthen your foundation. Here, on the day of Tiferet be-Yesod, balance between kindness and strength, we can find another sort of balance, that between our inside, thinking/feeling selves and our outside, experiencing/behaving selves.

In the quote for today, the philosopher Kierkegaard reminds us that even though we often believe that happiness will come to us from the physical world — an ice cream cone or a new toy, perhaps — it usually turns out that we are happiest when our insides are happy, whether that is because of the love of our family, a sense of pride in a big accomplishment, or because we know ourself deeply. As with every Tiferet day, or even any day at all, the secret is in the balance.

Try This:

Tomorrow morning, when you wake up, before your mind gets cluttered, try to catch yourself at peace, just as you are. Spend a little time in this half-waking time to notice the feeling of lightness. You are not yet weighed down by the rest of the world; all you are doing in these moments is existing. Try to remain in this state for a few minutes. Whatever happens during the course of your day, your core, your most essential self, is safe in your own care. You may choose to make this morning check-in a habit.

Today is the thirty-ninth day, making five weeks and four days of the Omer

Victory within Foundation
Netzach be-Yesod

הַיוֹם תִּשְׁעָה וּשְׁלשִׁים יוֹם שֶׁהֵם חֲמִשָּׁה שָׁבוּעוֹת וְאַרְבָּעָה יָמִים לָעֹמֶר

נֶצַח שֶׁבִּיסוֹד

Self-worth comes from one thing: thinking that you are worthy.

—Wayne Dyer

If you have a sense of self-worth, then you know your ideas are worthwhile, and you will express them with confidence and clarity. If you do not feel worthy, then you may squash your creativity before it ever sees the light of day, saying to yourself, "Well, it doesn't really matter," or, "No one would have listened anyway." Who knows what amazing things might be lost? Give yourself permission to be inventive and creative without censoring yourself.

Art Therapy:

Tonight and tomorrow, gather images and words from magazines, catalogs, websites, photo albums, etc., that reflect a way in which you have changed or something that you have learned about yourself as you have been counting the Omer and thinking about the Sefirot. If there is something which can not easily be added to a collage itself, then make a photocopy, take a picture and print it, or maybe even just draw it. Spend the time collecting and planning tonight and tomorrow with the goal of taking time tomorrow evening (or after Shabbat if the day falls on Friday to Saturday) to create a collage.

This does not need to be a masterpiece; think of it more as a visual collection of the ideas you've been exploring. You can keep it private or public as you wish. One thing you may want to do is to put it away in this book to rediscover next year and see how things have changed for you.

Today is the fortieth day, making five weeks and five days of the Omer

Glory within Foundation
Hod be-Yesod

הַיּוֹם אַרְבָּעִים יוֹם
שֶׁהֵם חֲמִשָּׁה שָׁבוּעוֹת
וַחֲמִשָּׁה יָמִים לָעֹמֶר

הוֹד שֶׁבִּיְסוֹד

If you think of feelings you have when you are awed by something — for example, knowing that elements in your body trace to exploded stars — I call that a spiritual reaction, speaking of awe and majesty, where words fail you.

—Neil deGrasse Tyson

The rabbi-mystics of centuries ago held the idea that each of us has sparks of the Divine within us made from the first light that God created when creating our universe. Dr. Tyson's spiritual/scientific observation hints that the rabbis understood the nature of the universe more realistically than many people give them credit for. Whether you consider it to be 'Divine sparks' or 'elements of exploded stars,' it is pretty awesome to imagine yourself cosmically connected to an ancient source. Many of us spend far too much time focusing on the worries of the moment. It is healthy to take the time to step back and marvel that we are made of amazing stuff and that our simple existence on earth is miraculous all by itself.

...continued from Last Night:

Spend time tonight craftting the collage from last night. Feel free to include words from headlines in the paper, pictures of animals from a magazine, even advertising flyers, if that is what is on your mind right now. The important thing at this point in our counting is to give yourself as much freedom as you can to be creative in expressing your mental and emotional processes.

If you are able, after reading the quote from Neil deGrasse Tyson, you might also want to get outside after dark, look to the sky, and experience some additional inspiration from his words.

Today is the forty-first day, making five weeks and six days of the Omer

הַיּוֹם אֶחָד וְאַרְבָּעִים יוֹם
שֶׁהֵם חֲמִשָּׁה שָׁבוּעוֹת
וְשִׁשָּׁה יָמִים לָעֹמֶר

Foundation within Foundation
Yesod be-Yesod

יְסוֹד שֶׁבִּיסוֹד

There is nothing either good or bad but thinking makes it so.

—William Shakespeare

Yesod be-Yesod is the distillation of all we have seen and experienced in our lives so far, how those things have shaped us and how we have grown as a response. Like plants, our basic inclination is to grow toward the light. When we live in a way that is healthy and balanced, we lean toward things that are to our benefit and avoid things that harm us. But it is not usually so simple, our lives are much more complex than that. Most situations are not simply good or bad; they are usually good in moderation, painful now, but will have a beneficial result, or a similar point on the spectrum between good and bad.

Finding our foundation means digging into that complexity and finding our boundaries within it. For example, a little chocolate is tasty but too much is unhealthy; exercise is good for our body and mind but too much can be harmful. Throughout our lives we are challenged to maintain balance, attending to it, and learning for ourselves what keeps us solid, grounded and whole.

Notes for Change:

Spend some time tonight (together if possible, or on your own) thinking of some beneficial choices that you aspire to make, (e.g. going to sleep earlier, healthier eating habits). As you hold one of these in your mind, imagine yourself doing it, and try to notice what thoughts or feelings within you are resisting.

Choose one to three of these goals, write them down and make notes about what gets in the way of your accomplishing them, (the resistant thoughts and feelings you experienced). Pick just one of these goals and make a conscious decision that from the strength within you, you are committing to acting on this one goal for a week. When you slip a little, just get back to it. Try not to give up for just one week.

WEEK 6 - YESOD

Today is the forty-second day, making six weeks of the Omer

הַיּוֹם שְׁנַיִם וְאַרְבָּעִים יוֹם שֶׁהֵם שִׁשָּׁה שָׁבוּעוֹת לָעֹמֶר

Majesty within Foundation
Malchut be-Yesod

מַלְכוּת שֶׁבִּיְסוֹד

To give real service you must add something which cannot be bought or measured with money, and that is sincerity and integrity.

—Douglas Adams

The basic majesty of humans is not just that we think, but that, having had many different ideas and plans, we can choose what we act on — what we decide to do or not to do. In concluding the week of Yesod, we continue to notice and examine our inner core being, our Yesod, through the lens of Malchut by watching ourselves in action. The sefirah of Malchut, with its focus on action and interaction, will be our focus for the entire coming week, as we come to the end of this cycle of counting the Omer culminating in our celebration of the holiday of Shavuot.

Malchut be-Yesod, majesty within foundation, is expressed above in the idea of sincerity driven by integrity. It is not enough to have integrity and know your inner foundation, but you must behave with great sincerity in order to make your greatest imprint on world. It is the sincerity and integrity with which we live our daily lives that brings our unique gifts into actuality.

Family Discussion:

With the final days of this year's journey in sight, it is time to look back at the ways in which our journey has affected our interactions with others. In what ways has your greater awareness of all of the unique feelings and skills that you embody affected the way you behave? What do you see in other people that you may not have been aware of or cared about before?

The root of the Hebrew word Malchut, majesty, is a homonym for the Hebrew word Malach, angel/messenger. When you think of these two concepts, what connections do you see? Is it possible that each of us carries an important message, without which the world would be dimished?

Week 7 – The Week of Malchut

Death is not the biggest fear we have;
  our biggest fear is taking the risk to be alive -
  the risk to be alive and express what we really are.

—Miguel Angel Ruiz

In the week of Yesod, we noticed the traits that are integral to each one of us individually, where our foundations and boundaries are, and how they are affected by the aspects of kindness and strength, beauty and victory, and glory. This final week of Sefirat haOmer is where the rubber meets the road. How do we take our timeless, integral self out into the world of interactions with others in which events happen, time passes and responses must be appropriate? The simple translation of Malchut is majesty, but that does not really capture the essence of the idea when we encounter it in the context of the sefirot, where it is often represented as 'the kiss of God', the place where, or moment when, the ephemeral Divine connects to the solid, time-bound reality of the world in which we walk.

All of the introspection and effort that we have brought to bear on ourselves culminates in this week of heightened awareness of our actions and how they affect those around us. We are the only creatures on the planet able to experience an event and then to think about, relive, and reframe the experience for a better understanding. Other animals may have feelings — certainly they have sensations — but they cannot take the pain they experience and understand that it is temporary and will pass. An animal experiencing pain cannot see past it, and only fights or endures it without being able to see a future in which it will live without that pain.

How will we, with our ability to conceive of a better future, aspire and act in ways that serve our vision?

Today is the forty-third day, making six weeks and one day of the Omer

הַיּוֹם שְׁלֹשָׁה וְאַרְבָּעִים יוֹם שֶׁהֵם שִׁשָּׁה שָׁבוּעוֹת וְיוֹם אֶחָד לָעֹמֶר

Kindness within Majesty
Hesed be-Malchut

חֶסֶד שֶׁבְּמַלְכוּת

Goodness is about character - integrity, honesty, kindness, generosity, moral courage, and the like.
More than anything else,
    it is about how we treat other people.

—Dennis Prager

It is very easy to sit comfortably in our seats and imagine ourselves to be kind and compassionate human beings. But the purpose of the whole sefirah journey, and especially in this week of Malchut, is to put our grand ideas into action.

We start with Hesed, as we have every week, reaching for the Hesed to consistently treat those around us kindly. All of our philosophy and religious imaginings are fruitless if they do not lead us directly to engaging in gentler and more generous interactions every day.

Words into actions:

Kindness   Goodness   Patience   Generosity

We have looked a various words at different times through this journey. Tonight, give some thought to these words, which are typical descriptions of Hesed. Is there one that draws you in, or one that you feel you connect with more than the others?

As you go through your day, think about living in Hesed be-Malchut — expressing Hesed through the way you act. Try to bring more Hesed into the world through your own behavior.

Today is the forty fourth day, making six weeks and two days of the Omer

Strength within Majesty
Gevurah be-Malchut

הַיוֹם אַרְבָּעָה וְאַרְבָּעִים יוֹם שֶׁהֵם שִׁשָּׁה שָׁבוּעוֹת וּשְׁנֵי יָמִים לָעֹמֶר

גְּבוּרָה שֶׁבְּמַלְכוּת

Courage is what it takes to stand up and speak; courage is also what it takes to sit down and listen.

—Winston Churchill

In the first week of Hesed, we considered the characteristic of Gevurah as a way of being kind by holding back. Sometimes our impulse to be kind unintentionally takes away some of the other person's ability to act on their own behalf, and is ultimately not as kind as we think.

When we look at Gevurah be-Malchut, we can imagine a different kind of restraint. As humans, we like to 'do something' in order to 'accomplish something'. We seem designed to be creatures of action, which is usually a good thing. But there are times when the strongest thing we can do is to sit still and listen to someone. Not just sit quietly while they talk, but to actively listen to what they are saying, to give it our full attention, to *be* with that person exclusively in that moment.

This kind of Gevruah is a skill that takes a lot of time to acquire; even people who are really good at it sometimes need to be reminded to use it. Our complete attention is a gift of strength that we can give to others in our life; it is one of the most valuable treasures we have to offer.

True Strength:

Be on the look-out for opportunities to demonstrate this most elemental form of Malchut through focused attention. When you are in a conversation try to be fully *in* that conversation and responsive to the person you are with. Resist the impulse to pull out an electronic device, and try not to let your thoughts wander off to other things.

With practice this will become easier and you will do it more frequently; you will have greatly expanded your capacity for Gevurah.

WEEK 7 - MALCHUT

Today is the forty-fifth day, making six weeks and three days of the Omer

הַיּוֹם חֲמִשָּׁה וְאַרְבָּעִים יוֹם
שֶׁהֵם שִׁשָּׁה שָׁבוּעוֹת
וּשְׁלֹשָׁה יָמִים לָעֹמֶר

Beauty within Majesty
Tiferet be-Malchut

תִּפְאֶרֶת שֶׁבְּמַלְכוּת

I call it sacred geometry. When everything's just right and it feels really balanced, so that when it unfolds to the next part, you feel totally familiar and at ease within the song.

—Jason Mraz

Music can find ways into our soul, even when words fail us. The Hasidim have long known that wordless tunes, niggunim, which circle back on themselves, the same simple tune repeated; sometimes slowly, sometimes quickly, growing louder or softer, quicker or slower, so the extended singing tells an entire emotional journey. Niggunim allow for a flowing musical expression of wordless feeling that can sometimes be more meaningful that the most artfully composed prayer. Jason Mraz calls it sacred geometry. Like meaningful music, Tiferet be-Malchut is the ability to find balance as you walk through the world and not lose sight of the *you* you most want to be, even in heated moments.

Tiferet be-Malchut is that core balance that can exist within you. Draw upon it, and bring some of that 'sacred flow' into the world as you go about doing your ordinary tasks.

Try This:

Singing or humming is a great way to express what is in your heart when it is hard to find words. When you make music, whether vocal or instrumental, you can feel transcendence — music has amazing power.

The next time you find yourself in search of Tiferet in your world, try humming or singing. It can be any melody that comes to mind. You may feel a little awkward in the beginning, but then, as you warm up and you begin to relax, you may find the Tiferet you were looking for. This practice can be one more tool in your 'spiritual toolbox' of ways to feel more connected to the essential good in the world when you find yourself feeling adrift.

Today is the forty-sixth day, making six weeks and four days of the Omer

הַיּוֹם שִׁשָּׁה וְאַרְבָּעִים יוֹם שֶׁהֵם שִׁשָּׁה שָׁבוּעוֹת וְאַרְבָּעָה יָמִים לָעֹמֶר

Victory within Majesty
Netzach be-Malchut

נֶצַח שֶׁבְּמַלְכוּת

Be willing to have it so. Acceptance of what has happened is the first step to overcoming the consequences of any misfortune.

—William James

Everybody has easier and harder times. As we draw closer to the re-experience of revelation of Sinai, and as we look past the counting of the Omer, it is worthwhile to think carefully about how we view misfortune, or difficult situations, in which we find ourselves.

These are moments when we have an opportunity to meet the world with Netzach, resilience, the ability to withstand adversity with our souls intact. Netzach has nothing whatever to do with 'beating the other guy.' It is about rising to our best, most heroic, selves when we might perhaps wish to ignore or hide from a bad situation or walk away from a challenge. To live with Netzach be-Malchut is to meet challenges with a clear sense of self and the knowledge that, while you might not always 'win,' you will always prevail so long as you maintain your integrity.

Notes for Change:

We spend so much time trying to do three things at once, that we often lose sight of the importance of focusing on one thing, or one person. Single-minded focus, though, can be quite an amazing tool.

As you go through your day(s), try to sense when someone would benefit from your full attention. This is a tool you should try to carry with you regularly. When it comes up that someone needs you, take a moment to push away as many distractions as possible (phone, computer and the like) and give them your full attention. You may be surprised by how much your full attention can mean.

WEEK 7 - MALCHUT

Today is the forty-seventh day, making six weeks and five days of the Omer

Glory within Majesty
Hod be-Malchut

הַיּוֹם שִׁבְעָה וְאַרְבָּעִים יוֹם
שֶׁהֵם שִׁשָּׁה שָׁבוּעוֹת
וַחֲמִשָּׁה יָמִים לָעֹמֶר

הוֹד שֶׁבְּמַלְכוּת

You are a child of God. Your playing small does not serve the world. There is nothing enlightened about shrinking so that other people won't feel insecure about you. We were born to manifest the glory of God that is within us.

—Marianne Williamson

The idea that humans are created in the image of God is one of the beliefs so ingrained in Jewish life that it is recited every morning in the daily liturgy. There are many subtly different ways of understanding this, but every one of them expresses the basic concept that humans carry within them the Divine spark, whatever we understand that to be. We have spoken of recognizing and honoring the Divine in those we encounter. It is more difficult to truly believe that we ourselves are made of Divine stuff. We do not make others greater by denying our own essential eternal internal flame. In fact, we lift others up when we express ourselves in ways that communicate the message, "I am worthy, and I know that you, too, are worthy." We give others a beautiful gift when we let them know that we believe in ourselves as much as we believe in them.

In Your Life:

Spend some time this evening thinking about how you treat yourself. Are you compassionate? Do you treat your body with care, building healthy habits for eating, exercise, study, rest and community, as well as solo time?

Do not begrudge the effort it takes to look after yourself in all of these areas; you are a complex being with many different needs, including the need to cut loose a little. So be moderate in all things, but also give yourself permission for the occasional indulgence. When you do not feel well, do what you need to do to feel better, rather than pretending you feel fine.

Things are ways of honoring the Divine spark within you and showing respect for the completely miraculous and unique self that you are.

In the spirit of Hod be-Malchut, write three things you can do to honor the inherent Hod within you. When you step out into the world, these small kindnesses toward yourself will shine through in subtle shifts of your comfort and ease out in the world.

To honor the Hod within myself, I will:

1.

2.

3.

Today is the forty-eighth day, making six weeks and six days of the Omer

Foundation within Majesty
Yesod be-Malchut

הַיּוֹם שְׁמוֹנָה וְאַרְבָּעִים יוֹם שֶׁהֵם שִׁשָּׁה שָׁבוּעוֹת וְשִׁשָּׁה יָמִים לָעֹמֶר

יְסוֹד שֶׁבְּמַלְכוּת

Individual commitment to a group effort — that is what makes a team work, a company work, a society work, a civilization work.
—Vince Lombardi

It is really a very simple idea – if you take all of the talent, imagination, drive, etc., that are at the core of your being and commit to being a part of something greater than you, then two things happen: you enrich the group, and the group enriches you. When you see and believe that you have something important and special to add, then your connection with others in the world around you is much stronger and more positive.

Yesod Check-in:

Last week, we initiated a week-long "yesod-oriented" practice:

Make some notes for yourself about what your goals are, (no more than 3), and what things are getting in your way, (the resistance thoughts and feelings you experienced). Pick just one of these goals and make a conscious choice that from the strength within you, you are committing to this one thing for a week. If you slip a little, just get back to it, but try not to give up just until next week, we'll check in then.

What was/were your goal(s)?

What got in your way? What resistance to working toward the goal(s) did you feel inside yourself? (Think of excuses you may have made: 'I'm too tired, too busy, not ready…')

How did you try to get past the resistance?

Were there times or circumstances when working toward your goal(s) was easier than others? What seemed to make the difference?

The goal(s) you chose: do you still want to work toward it/them? If not, how would you change it/them?

Today is the forty-ninth day, making seven weeks of the Omer

הַיּוֹם תִּשְׁעָה וְאַרְבָּעִים יוֹם שֶׁהֵם שִׁבְעָה שָׁבוּעוֹת לָעֹמֶר

Majesty within Majesty
Malchut be-Malchut

מַלְכוּת שֶׁבְּמַלְכוּת

The only limit to your impact is your imagination and commitment.

—Tony Robbins

This is the last day of counting. Do you feel ready to apply all of this exploration to developing your spiritual life? How will you continue to bring these ideas and questions into your life?

Malchut be-Malchut: the sefirah within a sefirah where all of our spiritual seeking is brought into existence through our behavior and interactions. We have spent these forty-nine days traveling together, preparing to celebrate Shavuot and re-experience revelation at Mount Sinai tomorrow! Next year, we may count this same cycle of sefirot, yet they will not be at all the same; each question you ask yourself will feel different because you will be different and the issues with which you will be wrestling will be different.

Looking Back on the Journey:
Review and reflect on the journey you have taken over these past 49 days.
What is different in how you view your life now?
Has the practice of examining small, focused aspects of your being affected the whole?
How?
Did you have a favorite day or exercise?
What will you carry with you as you continue to move forward?

Day 50 – Shavuot

Find your place on the planet, dig in,
and take responsibility from there.

—Gary Snyder

Tonight the sefirah journey is complete for the year. We will return to it next year, when the same questions will elicit different answers. We will have different concerns and other issues on our minds; we will have grown and changed in our approach to even the same issues.

The nature of the Jeiwish calendar and the holidays and even the cycle of reading the Torah underscores something about human nature: We cycle around repeatedly to the things with which we need to deal. Each time we get a little closer to resolution, and since we have grown and changed, we may have different answers to the same questions.

This, perhaps, is the trait that makes us least like the angels. For angels, who never wonder, never misbehave, and never get it wrong, the answers are always the same. Angels, as presented in rabbinic lore, do not grow or learn.

The author of the Psalms asks, "Who are humans, that you give us any thought? You have made us slightly less than angels…" "Slightly less"…, and yet so much more interesting and interactive. Though we may be lower than angels in a Divine hierarchy, still, we are valued because we question and grow. And so we are given the holiday cycle, the constant of the same words from the Torah scroll in year-long cycles, and this journey to travel each year, always asking the questions and learning by trial and error. We are not wandering, and we are not alone; we have a map, and we have the community of our fellow travelers. The journey continues next year….

With the holiday of Shavuot, we step off of the seven-by-seven cycle that we have followed since Passover. We enter uncharted territory for the first time in seven weeks, with no specific instructions or guidance about tending to our spiritual lives. From here, it is up to us to create both the questions and the answers. Shavuot is like an eternal eighth day because it is the day after a series of seven days of a sort of creation. Where we go from here and what we choose to do is entirely in our own hands.

Appendix: Kavvanot Meditations

There are a number of written kavanot (intentions) that some people add in order to enhance their concentration and focus. You may choose one or more to be a regular part of your counting ritual, or you may choose to vary them in order to make the practice of Sefirat HaOmer most meaningful to you.

1) For the unification

This kavanah is usually recited before counting of the day. It expresses the hope that by the action of doing this positive mitzvah we can have a part in repairing the world and unifying the name/existence of God:

לְשֵׁם יְחוּד קוּדְשָׁא בְּרִיךְ הוּא וּשְׁכִינְתֵּהּ בִּדְחִילוּ וּרְחִימוּ לְיַחֵד שֵׁם י״ה בו״ה בְּיִחוּדָא שְׁלִים בְּשֵׁם כָּל יִשְׂרָאֵל.

הִנְנִי מוּכָן וּמְזֻמָּן לְקַיֵּם מִצְוַת עָשֵׂה שֶׁל סְפִירַת הָעוֹמֶר כְּמוֹ שֶׁכָּתוּב בַּתּוֹרָה. וּסְפַרְתֶּם לָכֶם מִמָּחֳרַת הַשַּׁבָּת מִיּוֹם הֲבִיאֲכֶם אֶת עֹמֶר הַתְּנוּפָה שֶׁבַע שַׁבָּתוֹת תְּמִימֹת תִּהְיֶינָה. עַד מִמָּחֳרַת הַשַּׁבָּת הַשְּׁבִיעִת תִּסְפְּרוּ חֲמִשִּׁים יוֹם. וְהִקְרַבְתֶּם מִנְחָה חֲדָשָׁה לַיהוָֹה. וִיהִי נֹעַם אֲדֹנָי אֱלֹהֵינוּ עָלֵינוּ וּמַעֲשֵׂה יָדֵינוּ כּוֹנְנָה עָלֵינוּ, וּמַעֲשֵׂה יָדֵינוּ כּוֹנְנֵהוּ:

For the sake of unifying the Holy Blessed One and the Divine Presence in love and awe.

To unify the name of י״ה with the name of ו״ה in perfect unity in the name of all Israel,

Here I am, ready to engage in the positive mitzvah of Counting the Omer, as it is written in the Torah, "You shall count seven complete weeks from the day following the (Passover) rest day, when you brought the Omer as an offering. Until the day after the seventh week you shall count fifty days. Then you shall offer a new meal-offering to Adonai."

May we experience the grace of Adonai our God, and may the work of our hands reflect well upon us, and may the work of our hands honor God.

These next two are generally recited after the counting of the day.

They similarly expand in directing your intention that this act of counting not be mere words, but that somehow, through your words and focus you can effect change in yourself, and through that, be an agent of repair for the world.

2) Ana bikoach - By The Greatness of the Power

This kavvanah is also recited by some as a part of the Kabbalat Shabbat service. There are seven lines, each of which could be associated with one of the weeks or one of the Sefirot. Overall, it is a plea to God and a reminder to ourselves that we can only do our best as humans, and after that, the rest is out of our hands.

אָנָּא בְּכֹחַ גְּדֻלַּת יְמִינְךָ, תַּתִּיר צְרוּרָה.
קַבֵּל רִנַּת עַמְּךָ, שַׂגְּבֵנוּ, טַהֲרֵנוּ, נוֹרָא.
נָא גִבּוֹר דּוֹרְשֵׁי יִחוּדְךָ, כְּבָבַת שָׁמְרֵם.
בָּרְכֵם טַהֲרֵם, רַחֲמֵם צִדְקָתְךָ, תָּמִיד גָּמְלֵם.
חֲסִין קָדוֹשׁ, בְּרוֹב טוּבְךָ, נַהֵל עֲדָתֶךָ.
יָחִיד גֵּאֶה לְעַמְּךָ פְּנֵה, זוֹכְרֵי קְדֻשָּׁתֶךָ,
שַׁוְעָתֵנוּ קַבֵּל, וּשְׁמַע צַעֲקָתֵנוּ, יוֹדֵעַ תַּעֲלֻמוֹת

בָּרוּךְ שֵׁם כְּבוֹד מַלְכוּתוֹ לְעוֹלָם וָעֶד.

Please, by the greatness of the power of Your right hand,
  release those who are bound up.
Accept the prayer and song of Your people — Awesome One,
  strengthen and purify us.
Please, Mighty One, guard those who would unify You.
Bless them, purify them, have compassion for them,
  through Your righteousness support them.
Mighty One, Holy One, though Your abundant goodness,
  guide Your followers.
Only One, Exalted One, turn toward Your people,
  those who remember Your holiness.
Accept our plea, and hear our cries,
  You who know all secret thoughts.

Blessed be the Name of the Holy One forever and always.

3) Ribono she olam - Guardian of the Universe

This kavanah is unique to this particular mitzvah, and can help you to reflect on the internal work that you are doing in the course of counting.

רִבּוֹנוֹ שֶׁל עוֹלָם, אַתָּה צִוִּיתָנוּ עַל יְדֵי מֹשֶׁה עַבְדְּךָ לִסְפּוֹר
סְפִירַת הָעוֹמֶר כְּדֵי לְטַהֲרֵנוּ
מִקְּלִפּוֹתֵינוּ וּמִטֻּמְאוֹתֵינוּ. כְּמוֹ שֶׁכָּתַבְתָּ בְּתוֹרָתֶךָ:
וּסְפַרְתֶּם לָכֶם מִמָּחֳרַת הַשַּׁבָּת
מִיּוֹם הֲבִיאֲכֶם אֶת עוֹמֶר הַתְּנוּפָה שֶׁבַע שַׁבָּתוֹת תְּמִימוֹת תִּהְיֶינָה,
עַד מִמָּחֳרַת הַשַּׁבָּת הַשְּׁבִיעִית תִּסְפְּרוּ חֲמִשִּׁים יוֹם, כְּדֵי
שֶׁיִּטָּהֲרוּ נַפְשׁוֹת עַמְּךָ יִשְׂרָאֵל מִזֻּהֲמָתָם.
וּבְכֵן יְהִי רָצוֹן מִלְּפָנֶיךָ יְיָ אֱלֹהֵינוּ וֵאלֹהֵי אֲבוֹתֵינוּ,
שֶׁבִּזְכוּת סְפִירַת הָעוֹמֶר שֶׁסָּפַרְתִּי הַיּוֹם, יְתֻקַּן מַה שֶּׁפָּגַמְתִּי בִּסְפִירָה
{Insert Sefirot for the Day Here}
וְאֶטָּהֵר וְאֶתְקַדֵּשׁ בִּקְדֻשָּׁה שֶׁל מַעְלָה, וְעַל יְדֵי זֶה יֻשְׁפַּע שֶׁפַע רַב בְּכָל הָעוֹלָמוֹת וּלְתַקֵּן
אֶת נַפְשׁוֹתֵינוּ, וְרוּחוֹתֵינוּ וְנִשְׁמוֹתֵינוּ
מִכָּל סִיג וּפְגַם וּלְטַהֲרֵנוּ וּלְקַדְּשֵׁנוּ בִּקְדֻשָּׁתְךָ הָעֶלְיוֹנָה, אָמֵן סֶלָה:

    Guardian of the universe, You have commanded us through Moses, Your servant, to count the Omer in order to purify ourselves from our shards[*], shells and impurities.

    As You wrote in Your Torah, "You shall count seven complete weeks from the day following the (Passover) rest day, when you brought the Omer as an offering. Until the day after the seventh week you shall count fifty days. Then you shall offer a new meal-offering to Adonai.", in order to purify the souls of Your people Israel from all that might soil them.

    May it be Your will, Adonai our God and God of our ancestors, that through the merit of counting this day of the Omer, I will progress in repairing {*the combination of Sefirot for this day*}, and I will be cleansed and made holier through the experience of a bit of Your Holiness, and that through this process, there will flow a rich outpouring throughout all worlds, which will help to repair all of our souls, spirits and hearts from anything that is weighing us down, and will purify us and make us holier through the experience of contact with Divine Holiness.

---

[*] The Hebrew word 'klipot' is literally translated as 'shards' or 'shells' and refers to the mystical idea that there are fragments of primordial chaos and bad intent the identifying and discarding of which is our life-work in order to repair the world and bring about a Messianic Age of righteousness and peace.

APPENDIX: KAVVANOT MEDITATIONS

4) Psalm 67

Some people also include Psalm 67 in their reflections:

לַמְנַצֵּחַ בִּנְגִינֹת, מִזְמוֹר שִׁיר

אֱלֹהִים, יְחָנֵּנוּ וִיבָרְכֵנוּ; יָאֵר פָּנָיו אִתָּנוּ סֶלָה

לָדַעַת בָּאָרֶץ דַּרְכֶּךָ; בְּכָל-גּוֹיִם, יְשׁוּעָתֶךָ

יוֹדוּךָ עַמִּים אֱלֹהִים: יוֹדוּךָ, עַמִּים כֻּלָּם

יִשְׂמְחוּ וִירַנְּנוּ, לְאֻמִּים

כִּי-תִשְׁפֹּט עַמִּים מִישֹׁר; וּלְאֻמִּים, בָּאָרֶץ תַּנְחֵם סֶלָה

יוֹדוּךָ עַמִּים אֱלֹהִים: יוֹדוּךָ, עַמִּים כֻּלָּם

אֶרֶץ, נָתְנָה יְבוּלָהּ; יְבָרְכֵנוּ, אֱלֹהִים אֱלֹהֵינוּ

יְבָרְכֵנוּ אֱלֹהִים; וְיִירְאוּ אוֹתוֹ, כָּל-אַפְסֵי-אָרֶץ

For the chief musician for stringed instruments, A Psalm Song.
God be gracious to us, and bless us; and let his face shine upon us, Selah.
That Your way may be known on earth, Your salvation among all nations.
Let the peoples praise You, O God; let all the peoples praise You.
O let the nations be glad and sing for joy; for you shall judge the peoples equally, and lead the nations of the earth.
Let the nations thank You, O God, let all the nations thank You.
The earth has yielded her abundance, let God, our Sovereign, bless us.
God shall bless us; let all the ends of the earth stand in awe of Him.

Acknowledgements

Judaism encourages us to create joy in our lives, to form communities and to gain strength from these relationships. I believe that Judaism is a religion of "yes" far more than a religion of "no." We shine a light on the positive acts in Jewish practice each time we recite a blessing thanking God for giving us a mitzvah to perform. In this way, we focus on the positive Jewish practices in our lives every day. I have traveled a long way from frustration with seemingly meaningless restrictions on certain activities during the Omer into the positive approach that I describe in this book.

Among the numerous positive influences in my life that have shaped this book, I need to name a few in particular. First, my own children who provided me with a real-life "laboratory" to experiment and observe many of the things mentioned in these pages. The Beit Rabban Day School has been a welcoming environment where classroom observation and teaching has helped to shape several ideas. I am grateful to my parents, who raised me to question all assumptions, and who brought me into a synagogue environment where there was a rabbi who took the questions of a young congregant as seriously as he would those of an adult.

Of course no book happens until a publisher says "yes," and I am very grateful to Larry Yudelson for believing in the concept and including my work in the varied and interesting offerings of Ben Yehuda Press. And the last word goes to my editor and "wordsmith-in-chief" Rhonda Rosenheck, who combed through my manuscript with a very close eye and left no dot misplaced, as well as offering her wisdom in making my ideas sound clearer and more understandable than I had expressed them.

Lea Gavrieli
5776

www.ingramcontent.com/pod-product-compliance
Lightning Source LLC
LaVergne TN
LVHW061346060426
835512LV00012B/2584